Gourmet
Nutritional Therapy
Cookbook

- ◆ All recipes free from wheat, cow's milk, egg & yeast
- ◆ Many gluten-free recipes
- ◆ Rich in superfoods
- ◆ Many recipes suitable for vegetarians and vegans

LINDA LAZARIDES

School of Modern Naturopathy

Other works by Linda Lazarides
Principles of Nutritional Therapy
The Nutritional Health Bible
The Waterfall Diet
The Amino Acid Report
A Textbook of Modern Naturopathy
Linda's Flat Stomach Secrets
The Big Healthy Soup Diet
Easy Water Retention Diet

About the Author

Linda Lazarides has helped countless people return to good health. She is one of Britain's most respected natural health experts, author of eight books, founder of the British Association for Nutritional Therapy, and Principal of the School of Modern Naturopathy.

2nd Edition (revised and expanded)
©Linda Lazarides 2016
www.naturostudy.org

ISBN-13: 978-1450522342
ISBN-10: 1450522343

Published in the United Kingdom.

CONTENTS

Part II: Getting organized

Part III: Gourmet recipes

Appendices

Introduction

'You are what you eat' is such a cliché that we rarely stop to think about what it means. Most of us in fact are already convinced that we eat a healthy diet. Ask anybody you know and they will usually say 'Well, I probably eat a little bit too much chocolate (fried food, cake, ice cream, chips, sodas, candy, burgers, butter etc.) but otherwise my diet is healthy'.

If you were to ask this person to fill in the questionnaire used at the School of Modern Naturopathy, you may very well find that in fact they eat red or processed meat ten times a week, eat deep-fried foods five times a week, consume foods or drinks containing added sugar nine times a day, get a dose of high fructose corn syrup five times a week in soft drinks, and consume alcohol several times a week.

If this sounds like you, you may feel ok right now, but these habits are silently setting up your body for future problems. Most of these problems will be related to vitamin and mineral depletion; others will be related to developing internal body fat (the type which causes the 'apple shape' body) leading to insulin resistance and high cholesterol. The rest will be related to the formation of free radicals, which induce DNA damage—the cause of cancer. It's a Russian roulette situation with your genes in control of the gun. The wrong genes, and the harmful effects will come sooner than later. They may not kill you, but there truly is nothing like poor health to spoil our quality of life.

Another important cause of ill health is known as 'food intolerance'. Food intolerances produce unpleasant symptoms, and are similar to food allergies, though not life-threatening. You can read more about them on page 15. Most of the people who have food intolerances are intolerant to wheat, dairy products, eggs or yeast, which is why these foods are excluded from our recipes.

So what can this recipe book do for you? First of all, it uses foods that are rich in vitamins, minerals and 'superfood' factors that help to prevent and resist disease. It shows you how to drastically reduce sugar, sweeteners and corn syrup—the main causes of 'apple shape' fat. It avoids red and processed meat and deep frying, which favour free radical formation. By avoiding the main foods linked with food intolerances, it can provide relief for many common ailments—up to 30 per cent of all the cases for which physicians and GPs write prescriptions day after day for life.

I do hope this book will help you rethink what 'You are what you eat' really means. I have put a great deal of thought and care into making the recipes as delicious as possible, in the hope that you will enjoy as well as benefit from them.

If you are used to eating a very conventional diet, similar to one which most of us have grown up with, it is best to start with the recipes that you can work with straight away, e.g. using chicken or fish, rice, potatoes and fresh vegetables. This gives you time to find the best places to purchase less familiar ingredients, and learn how to use them. You can take your time over this. It is better to build up slowly to using more of the recipes, rather than take on too much too soon. You don't have to use all the ingredients, so don't be daunted if you don't like some, or if they are not easily available where you live.

Most of the less familiar ingredients can be found in health food stores. These stores are a great place to link up with other people who are looking for ways to improve their health. Ask about local clubs and societies, and soon you will meet many more people who are on a similar journey to yours. Their support and encouragement can be very helpful.

If you have a health problem that you need to work on, you will get the most rapid results by exclusively using ingredients listed in this book for a while. If you are working with a nutritional medicine doctor, a naturopath or a natural medicine practitioner, they may even recommend this.

This book is also useful if you have to cook for people with special dietary needs as many of the recipes are suitable for vegetarians, vegans and for those who follow a completely gluten-free diet.

Wishing you good health

Linda Lazarides

The School of Modern Naturopathy
London, United Kingdom

Part I
Food and Your Health

1. Nutritional therapy works!

Nutrition used to be a boring old subject. Gone are the days when all we worried about was fats, carbohydrate and protein. Modern nutrition covers everything from the cancer-protective effects of broccoli to the health benefits of oily fish and the humble bacteria found in yoghurt.

Is it really possible for nutrition to make a difference to your health? In fact, how well you feel depends on how efficiently your body produces essential enzymes, hormones and other substances, and gets rid of wastes and toxins that could interfere with your internal chemistry. Take a look at the charts opposite. These show the results achieved in one of the rare doctor's practices which uses nutritional medicine. The patients were all those referred to a nutritional therapist from 1990-1993.

Nutritional medicine or therapy, also known as naturopathy, simply means improving health by giving the body the nutrients it is lacking, improving its elimination of wastes, and removing food ingredients, chemicals or pollutants that may be stressing it. This is how the results on the opposite page were achieved.

Some doctors practise nutritional medicine or naturopathy, but if yours does not, or does not yet employ a nutritional therapist or naturopathic nutritionist, you can find many who work in private practice for very reasonable fees, and can provide the guidance you need.

Why these recipes?

The reason why the recipes in this book are free of wheat, dairy products, eggs and yeast, is that these are the foods most often responsible for hidden food 'intolerances'—sometimes known as food allergies. Food intolerances are not allergies in the strict sense of the word. They do not cause life-threatening reactions like a peanut allergy for instance. But they can cause many unpleasant, long-term health problems. If you are intolerant to a food such as wheat, and particles of this food that have not been completely digested get

Figure I: Results achieved with nutritional therapy in a GP practice

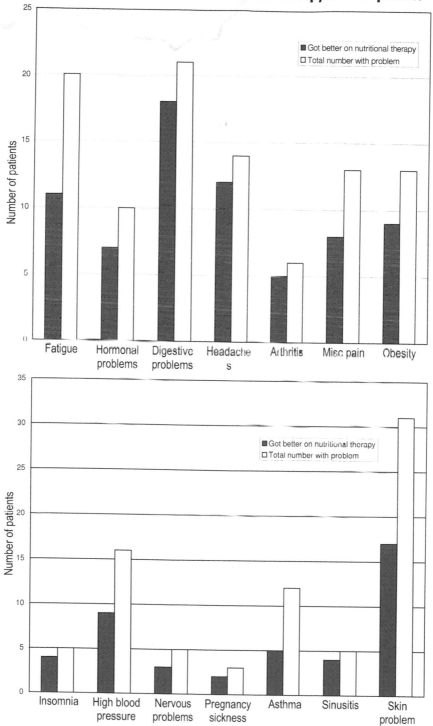

Linda Lazarides 1993

through your gut wall and come into contact with white cells in your blood, histamine is produced. Histamine causes inflammation, e.g. in the form of swellings after an insect bite, and redness and sneezing associated with hay fever. So you can imagine what symptoms it can cause when it travels in your blood to your internal organs:

- Migraine and headaches
- Congested sinuses
- Eczema and rashes
- Bloating
- Chronic fatigue or unexplained drowsiness
- Brain 'fog'
- Sudden bouts of unusual aggression or depression
- Behavioural problems in children, including hyperactive and autistic behaviour
- Diarrhoea or severe constipation or both (alternating)
- Griping tummy pains, with or without mucus discharge
- Painful or swollen joints
- Water retention (and resulting weight gain)
- Chronic catarrh
- Wheezing and breathing difficulties
- Rheumatic pains

Imagine also what happens if you eat the offending food several times every day. Lots of people eat toast for breakfast, sandwiches for lunch and pasta for dinner, not to mention biscuits, cookies or cake in between. If your problem food is wheat, then you could have one of these symptoms practically all the time. If wheat is not removed from your diet to give your body the chance to recover, you may never know that your arthritis, for instance, has anything to do with what you are eating.

The same applies if you develop an intolerance to cow's milk and dairy products. Just a few spoonfuls of milk in tea or coffee several times a day, plus the occasional portion of cheese or yoghurt, can keep your symptoms going forever. You won't feel particularly worse just after consuming the problem food. Symptoms usually come and go with no particular pattern. Migraine sufferers may get a migraine once every few days, or only when they are under stress. But take the problem food away, and stress on its own no longer brings on a migraine.

Doctors who specialize in nutritional medicine say that up to one third of all people who consult a family doctor for long-term ailments could be cured within a week by removing the foods they are intolerant to. This book provides lots of delicious recipes so that you can see how you feel if you avoid the most common intolerance-producing foods. Later on if you work with a naturopathic nutritionist or a doctor specializing in nutritional medicine, they will work with you to pinpoint the exact foods that are causing your symptoms.

It's worth persevering

If—like up to 30 per cent of people with a chronic ailment—you do have a food intolerance, try to give this recipe book a chance. It's not always easy to change our eating habits, even if only for a week, so focusing on the potential benefits is important.

Most people feel wonderful a few days after they stop eating a food to which they are intolerant. It is like gaining a new lease of life—a fabulous, rapid and totally unexpected freedom from pain and discomfort, and a new confidence as you regain control over your health. People too chronically exhausted to walk have become physically active again. Weekly migraines that always lasted 48 hours have vanished forever. Chronic sinus congestion has miraculously cleared. Bowels have begun to work normally again. Chronic eczema has disappeared. Burning rheumatic pains which the doctors cannot explain have melted away. Arthritic joints have stopped hurting. Waterlogged body tissues have given up years of retained fluid resulting in permanent weight loss of up to 10-15 lbs—the list goes on and on. I have personally seen all these results.

The foods that protect your health

The recipes in this book don't just avoid certain foods—they emphasize the foods that can help to enhance your health. We now know that many items act as 'superfoods'—foods which have extraordinary health benefits by being extra-rich in vitamins, minerals, antioxidants or flavonoids—components found in certain fruits and vegetables, which have powerful disease-fighting properties.

Hundreds of research studies now show that the more fruit and vegetables, whole grains, fish and fresh nuts and olive oil we consume in preference to other foods, the better our protection against major killer diseases. People who consume the least fruits and vegetables can have more than double the risk of contracting heart disease or cancer in later life. The protection given by a good diet is very significant indeed. The more brightly-coloured the fruit or vegetable—e.g. bright purple, orange, red or green—the better its protection, since it is the coloured parts which are the most rich in antioxidants and flavonoids.

Plant whole-foods are also rich in B vitamins, especially folic acid. Only in the last few years have scientists discovered that adults with a B vitamin deficiency can develop high levels of a toxin known as homocysteine, which accelerates cholesterol build-up in the arteries. We also know that the brittle bone disease (osteoporosis) which affects elderly people also seems to be greatly accelerated when homocysteine levels are high.

So don't just eat whole-grains and greens to 'keep you regular'— eat them to help protect your heart and your bones. In this book you will find information on the most effective superfoods, and more than 100 recipes to help you learn how to make delicious meals and snacks quickly and easily.

2. More about food intolerances

Unlike an allergy, which is usually inherited and with you for life, a food intolerance can develop quite suddenly. Nobody knows exactly what brings it on, but damage to the intestinal walls caused by chronic poor digestion and irritation is thought to play an important part. This damage makes the intestines 'leaky'.

When the intestinal wall becomes leaky, bits of partly-digested protein from your meal (known as peptides) leak through the walls of your digestive system into your bloodstream. This leakage of food should never normally occur. When it does, your immune system treats the peptides as if they were bacteria. It attaches antibodies to the peptides to make them easy targets for destruction. When these peptide/antibody complexes come into contact with histamine-producing white blood cells they stimulate them to release histamine.

Histamine is a chemical responsible for the physical symptoms experienced by allergy sufferers. If you have ever suffered from hay fever or insect bites, you will be familiar with some of its effects. Histamine dilates your blood capillaries, producing symptoms such as skin redness, swelling and irritation, and can also constrict the bronchi of the lungs, causing wheezing (asthma). Depending on which parts of the body it targets, histamine can cause any of the symptoms listed on page 12.

Foods responsible for food intolerance reactions

- **Wheat** (found in bread, flour, biscuits, cookies, sauces, etc.)
- **Dairy products** (found in milk, cream, cheese, yoghurt, butter, and anything containing these)
- **Egg** (found in egg dishes, egg pasta, many brands of ice cream, desserts, batter, pancakes etc.)
- **Yeast** (found in alcoholic drinks, stock cubes and other savoury flavourings, gravy mix, bread and pizza)

Soy, maize (corn), gluten (found in wheat, rye, barley, spelt and sometimes as a contaminant in oats) as well as nuts, citrus fruit, meats and tomatoes can sometimes be problem ingredients. Soy and corn are more likely to be problem foods in the United States than elsewhere, possibly by being more common there.

Gluten can be found in trace amounts in the meat of grain-fed animals, and if you have a gluten allergy or intolerance, it may be these traces of gluten rather than the meats themselves which cause your intolerant reactions.

If you have a food intolerance, the chances are that one of the four main foods listed above in bold type will be responsible. The symptoms are not caused by the food itself, but by your reaction to it. So one individual may develop headaches from eating bread; another may get catarrh. The symptoms often come and go at random, or they may be present most of the time. Although the list of potential symptoms is long, you will probably only have one or two symptoms, depending on which of your organs are your 'weakest link'.

Eat organic if you can

Wheat, dairy products, eggs and yeast do seem to be such common causes of food intolerance reactions that I usually advise people to consume them only in moderation even if they no longer cause symptoms. Modern wheat strains have been bred to have a very high gluten yield. Modern yeast strains have been bred to a very high degree of virulence. Commercial dairy cows and laying hens are often fed a rather unnatural diet, which may include yellow colouring to make cream and yolks look more appetizing. (Farmed fish can also be prone to chemical additives.) I would certainly recommend eating organic versions of wheat, dairy products and eggs. I have come across children who become hyperactive after drinking ordinary milk but not after drinking organic milk.

From my casebook

Lizzie

What I think a lot of people don't realize when they start on nutritional therapy is that it's not a starvation diet. You can eat lots of

really nice food. My problem was overweight, although I was only eating about 1,000 calories a day. Linda told me I could eat another 500 calories a day as long as I gave up two foods which she thought I could be allergic to. I did give them up and within three weeks I lost more than a stone* in weight despite the extra calories. The food allergy had been making me retain fluid. I looked fat, but I wasn't actually fat at all—it was all water, and it stayed away as long as I stayed off my problem foods
*14 lbs

Additional items

The recipes in this book also avoid the following items:

- Alcohol
- Artificial food additives
- Red meat and animal fat
- Hydrogenated and 'trans' fats
- Highly salted foods
- Sugar, syrup and honey

The reasons are as follows, and some healthy alternatives are given which you may find to be helpful substitutes.

Alcohol

Alcohol is toxic to every cell in your body. It stresses your liver and harmful toxins are created while it is being broken down. Alcohol also reduces the effectiveness of anti-diuretic hormone (ADH). When your body's fluid levels are getting low, you need this hormone to slow down your excretion of fluid. If it is not working properly you can go on rapidly excreting water even when you are already dehydrated.

ALTERNATIVES: Many people drink alcohol because it helps them relax. Chamomile tea is a good alternative relaxant. If missing the social element of drinking alcohol is a problem, you may want to consider widening your scope of social activities so that you can find other ways to enjoy your spare time.

Artificial food additives

It is hard to avoid these if we eat commercially manufactured foods. Almost everything contains a cocktail of additives: preservatives, colourings, artificial sweeteners, flavourings and flavour enhancers to name just a few. Sometimes the law does not even require additives to be listed on a packet. For instance a chilled meal purchased from a supermarket may appear to contain no additives at all, but this is because items like 'stock' (broth) do not have to declare small amounts of sub-ingredients they contain.

The problem with additives is that we only know if they harm the health of well-nourished laboratory animals given them singly in large quantities. We have no idea how they affect the health of humans when consumed over a lifetime in dozens of different combinations.

Large numbers of people are sensitive to these chemicals. For instance, sulphur-based preservatives may trigger asthma and digestive inflammation, and colourings can cause rashes or disturbed behaviour in some children. Certain colourings can react with bacteria in the intestines to form cancer-causing compounds. Additives originally thought safe to eat have later been banned. The sweetener aspartame, used as tablets and in countless 'diet' products such as yoghurt, cola and ice-cream and by diabetics is causing worries since being linked with headaches, memory loss, eye problems and seizures.

One thing we do know is that your liver must try to break down these foreign chemicals and uses up its precious resources in doing so. What we do not know is how successful *your* liver is in coping, and whether any toxins will linger in your system.

One of the greatest concerns about additives is the unknown effect of mixing them together as we eat different foods containing them.

ALTERNATIVES: There are now many additive-free products on the market. Health food stores often specialize in them. Or make your own additive-free food.

Bad fats

Fat is not a poison, and does not need to be avoided completely, although some people mistakenly treat it that way. In fact it is essential to have some fat (in the form of essential polyunsaturated oils) in your diet. But most of us eat far more bad fats than we realize since the fat in most high-fat foods is invisible. The fats which especially need to be controlled are animal fat and hydrogenated or partially hydrogenated fat.

Animal fat

Animal fat is sold as butter and lard and found in full-fat milk, minced or ground beef and burgers, sausages, pies, chocolate, ice cream, fried food, cream, cheese, eggs, cookies, English biscuits, cakes, desserts and pastries. Too much of these foods can encourage excess cholesterol in your blood, especially if you also consume a lot of sugar-rich food. Animal fat is mostly saturated fat—also known as hard fat because it is solid at room temperature.

Which fats should I eat?

Olive oil

Can be used in salads, dips, mayonnaise and for frying up to medium heat. if the olive oil will form part of the dish, use the very beneficial 'extra-virgin' variety, which is the very special first pressing of the olives, and is made without heating the oil. Use ordinary olive oil (which is cheaper) if it is only needed for frying.

Groundnut oil

Can also be used for frying, especially when the strong taste of olive oil is not wanted. Like olive oil, it is not rapidly damaged by heat.

Polyunsaturated oils

Sunflower, safflower, soy oil, flax seed oil, hemp oil, walnut oil—use only cold, for salad dressings, mayonnaise, dips etc.

Coconut Oil

Is hard at room temperature and so technically is a saturated fat. But studies have shown that it does not raise cholesterol like butter does. Use it for frying, pie-crusts, baking and cake-making. Coconut oil is also a traditional ingredient of many oriental dishes and curries. You can find it in larger supermarkets, health food stores and shops that specialize in Asian cookery.

While animal fat tends to consist of little more than calories, some hard fats derived from plants do also contain useful ingredients, for instance

- Sterols, found in a variety of plant fats and oils, block the absorption of cholesterol from your diet,
- Tocotrienols, found in palm oil/fat, have cholesterol-lowering properties,
- Isoflavones, found in many plant fats and oils, are good balancers of the female hormone oestrogen (estrogen) and can also help to prevent prostate cancer,
- Lauric acid, found in coconut milk and coconut oil or fat, can inactivate many viruses and bacteria. Due to its high content of medium chain triglycerides, the body does not treat coconut oil as fat. Instead of being deposited around the body it is used to make energy.

One of the dangers of consuming too much saturated animal fat is that the delicate outer membranes which cover our cells could become too rigid. This affects the ability of oxygen-carrying red blood cells to squeeze through narrow blood vessels (capillaries) in your brain, eyes, ears etc. Inflexible red cells can block your capillaries, leading to a poorer blood and oxygen supply to these sensitive areas, especially if you are an elderly person.

Hydrogenated fats

These are artificially hardened fats. You may find these listed as an ingredient on packets of biscuits, cookies, ice-cream and many processed or convenience foods. In some catering establishments foods are deep-fried in hydrogenated fats. Hydrogenated fats are oils which have been treated with hydrogen to make them hard at room temperature. Many brands of margarine, fats used for baking, and 'vegetable fats' are made in this way. Sometimes they are only partially hydrogenated, which reduces the hardness to a 'soft margarine' consistency. Recent research has linked a high consumption of partially hydrogenated fats with a higher risk of heart disease. Most types of margarine are artificially hardened fats.

'Trans' fats

Commercial processing of oils and fats frequently creates an unnatural type of fat molecule known as the 'trans' form. Once in your body, these trans fats can grab enzymes needed by essential fatty acids (EFAs). EFAs are similar to vitamins. They are derived from oily foods like nuts and sunflower seeds, and must be obtained from your food. Your body cannot manufacture them.

Essential fatty acids are especially needed by your cell membranes. They keep them supple and able to do their important job of aiding the entry of oxygen and nutrients into your cells and the exit of various waste products. So don't think that all fats are bad. The oily fats found in nuts and seeds are very beneficial indeed, although of course like any fatty or oily food you do have to watch out for the calorie content. Fortunately these naturally oily foods keep you feeling full for longer than carbohydrates, so they may help you to eat less.

If consuming too much trans fat prevents your body from using EFAs, it effectively means that a diet with too much highly processed fat or oil can in time produce the effects of an EFA deficiency even if you are consuming enough EFAs.

Effects of EFA deficiency include dry skin, premenstrual syndrome, increased susceptibility to inflammation, problems with your cell membranes, and microclots which can impede the circulation to your eyes, ears and brain.

Red meat

Red meat (even if apparently lean) and saturated fat contain arachidonic acid, which can encourage inflammation in your skin, joints or other parts of your body. The saturated fat in red meat contributes to developing cholesterol deposits in arteries. Curing and smoking meat, and browning it during during cooking gives rise to cancer-causing substances known as polycyclic aromatic hydrocarbons (PAHs).

Since PAHs are strongly linked with bowel cancer in particular, the World Health Organization has for many years recommended restricting the consumption of red and processed meats to no more than twice a week.

White meat (poultry) is much less fatty and so less likely to be a problem, but it is better if it has been organically raised. Even free-range chickens may be fed standard commercial feed which contains antibiotics, dung from other chickens, and other unsavoury items. We do not know how well a chicken's liver can cope with these challenges and what kind of residues remain in the bird's meat and fat.

Non-organic chickens are routinely fed antibiotics. The bacteria in the chicken's intestines can become resistant to them and the bacteria in humans who consume the birds can acquire this resistance. This has led to life-threatening cases where salmonella poisoning, for instance, becomes virtually untreatable because no antibiotic is effective.

Organic chickens are kept in much more humane, less overcrowded conditions, and do not need to be dosed daily with antibiotics as they are much less likely to develop infections.

ALTERNATIVES: Fish, nuts, beans, tofu. Nuts are an excellent protein source and very underrated. Rice can also contribute significant amounts of protein to your diet.

Salt

and sodium-rich foods, including:

1. Highly salted or smoked foods such as salami, ham and bacon, sausages, smoked fish, canned foods, salty cheeses, salted nuts, crisps and other packet snacks, bread, stock cubes, yeast extract, soy sauce and ready prepared pies, quiches, sauces, or commercially manufactured 'oven-ready' dishes.
2. Sodium-rich drinks, medicines and food additives. Baking powder. Most commercial soft drinks are very high in sodium. Some medicines, such as antacids based on bicarbonate of soda or effervescent tablets of any kind can also contain large amounts of sodium. One of the most common food additives is a flavour-enhancer known as mono*sodium* glutamate or (in UK/Europe) 'E621'. Other sodium-rich food additives are sodium benzoate, sodium metabisulphite, sodium nitrite, sodium nitrate, sodium

acetate, sodium propionate, sodium orthophosphate, sodium malate, sodium alginate, sodium polyphosphate, sodium carboxymethylcellulose, sodium carbonate, sodium sulphate, sodium hydroxide (caustic soda), sodium aluminum phosphate, sodium gluconate.

These foods, plus adding salt at the table can easily lead to a salt intake of 12-17 grams a day. The World Health Organization recommends no more than 5 grams.

A high salt intake has been linked with

- Water retention
- High blood pressure and weight gain (as a result of water retention)
- Osteoporosis (brittle bone disease)
- A worsening of asthma.

The best way to control salt is to eat food which you have prepared yourself, so you know exactly how much salt you have put in it. Low-sodium salt products are now available in supermarkets, and can help to cut your salt intake by 50 per cent or more. The recipes in this book will also help you to cut your salt intake drastically, but some use a little tamari sauce or miso, oriental flavourings which do contain salt but are also rich in other nutrients. If you have been placed on a totally salt-free diet you could omit these or use a salt substitute product instead.

Baking powder contains bicarbonate of soda, which has effects similar to those of salt.

Sugar, honey and syrup

Read the labels, since sugar is also known as *sucrose, glucose, dextrose, fructose and corn syrup.*

Sugar, a form of carbohydrate, is a natural component of fruit and vegetables, where it is not in concentrated form. Concentrated sugar is found in products such as honey, syrup and 'nectar', which are mainly sugar and water. The most concentrated form of sugar is the brown or white crystals we buy in packets, which are added to drinks or found in soda pops, ice cream, milk shakes, cakes, biscuits, cookies, jam,

> ## Did You Know?
>
> When advertisements for sugar claim that sugar 'gives you energy', they are not using the term 'energy' in the usual sense of the word—helping you to *feel* more energetic. All our energy needs can be met by consuming a normal diet containing no added sugar at all.
> In fact, energy is a scientific term for calories, so the ads are really just telling you that sugar will provide you with calories!

desserts, sweets and chocolate. In this form, the average person in the UK consumes about two pounds of sugar a week.

Most of us know that eating too much sugar is bad for our teeth and probably not good for our health. The big question is, how much is too much?

Let's look at it this way. We can only eat a certain number of calories a day without putting on excess weight. If one third of those calories come from sugar, you are eating only two thirds of the vitamin-rich food which a person on a low-sugar diet eats, since sugar consists of calories and no other nutrients. If you don't believe that one third or more of your diet consists of sugar, read on.

If you are consuming the national average of two pounds of sugar per week, that comes to about 150 grams a day. Each gram of sugar yields four kcal (Calories), making 600 Calories a day from sugar—or about one third of a normal calorie intake for a woman and one quarter of a normal calorie intake for a man.

Add to this the 30-40 per cent of our diet that comes from fat, and you can see how dangerously high your diet could be in 'empty' calories—that is to say foods which provide only calories and virtually no other nutrients at all.

Of course, a national average sugar consumption of two pounds a week means that most people will be consuming either more or less than this amount. If you know that you consume a lot of sugary foods and drinks, your total intake of empty calories could be as much as 80 per cent of your diet.

Your body is not going to react right away to being treated like this.

It is very good at coping silently. But in time you could develop vitamin and mineral deficiency symptoms, such as

- Skin problems
- Nervous problems
- Lacking energy and stamina
- Frequent infections
- Period pains or PMS
- Diabetes
- Enlarged prostate.

If your liver does not get enough vitamins and minerals to make essential enzymes, it could start to have difficulty processing wastes and pollutants, which in turn can lead to inflammation in your skin or joints, fluid retention, headaches, lethargy and accelerated ageing. A weakening of your immune system reduces your body's ability to protect itself against cancer.

Taking vitamin pills to compensate for the empty calories is not the solution—hundreds of medical studies are showing that the people with the highest *fruit and vegetable* consumption are those least likely to get cancer and heart disease. These foods contain a lot of important nutrients besides vitamins and minerals.

Added sugar—and this includes honey, syrup and 'nectar', which are also concentrated sugar—is absorbed very fast, making your insulin rise too quickly and too high. Scientific trials show that high insulin levels encourage high fat levels in your blood, and cholesterol deposits on your artery walls. As reported in *Pure White and Deadly,* a book about sugar written by the late professor of nutrition John Yudkin, your blood also becomes more 'sticky', and so prone to tiny clots that could lead to a heart attack as you get older. High insulin levels make you gain weight: you retain sodium, which encourages water retention, and you form body fat more easily, especially around your middle. This weight becomes very hard to lose.

It really is worth curbing your sweet tooth. Wouldn't you like to approach old age feeling fit and well rather than on a cocktail of medications for high cholesterol, high blood pressure and diabetes? Avoiding sugar does not have to mean going without sweet things. This book provides lots of recipes for delicious desserts—even chocolate mousse!

ALTERNATIVES: Use naturally sweet foods like bananas, raisins, dates and cashew nuts. These contain dietary fibre which helps slow down the absorption of the sugar they contain. When natural sugars are absorbed slowly, insulin 'spikes' are less likely to occur.

Tea and coffee

(including decaffeinated versions)

These have a diuretic effect. They make you urinate more, which encourages dehydration, and increased losses of magnesium and other minerals. Taken with meals, tea and coffee substantially reduce the absorption of iron and zinc from your food. This may account for why some researchers believe these drinks can encourage infertility.

Coffee is a nervous system stimulant which may provoke anxiety and panic attacks in susceptible people. It increases your liver's workload. Children who consume it regularly have an increased risk of diabetes.

ALTERNATIVES: Chamomile, peppermint, fennel tea, spice tea, lemon and ginger tea, chicory, dandelion coffee.

Wheat, cow's milk, eggs and yeast

All the recipes in this book are made with alternatives to these ingredients. Most of the recipes are also gluten-free, so can be used by those with a coeliac (celiac) problem.

3. A word about pollutants

It is hard to avoid external pollutants such as traffic fumes and contaminants found in our food and water, though we should be as vigilant as we can, since pollutants can build up and cause not just toxic reactions, but allergic reactions too. The pollutants in our homes are more controllable, and although we usually believe our homes are not polluted, in fact they often are, as you can see from the list below. Try to keep a window open, even if just a little, to improve air quality.

Everything that is inhaled through our lungs comes in contact with our nervous system, and has the potential to affect its delicate balance. Some individuals with severe chronic fatigue syndrome, for example, become very ill when exposed to tobacco smoke or room fresheners.

We can cut down on our exposure to pollutants by avoiding the items listed below, or using natural, gentle or organic alternatives.

Common chemical pollutants found in the home

Home care materials
Toilet cleaners
Oven cleaners
Spray polish
Artificial air fresheners
Carpet cleaners
Detergents, bleach
Fabric conditioners
Shoe & metal polish

Cosmetics and personal hygiene
Nail varnish & remover
Hair spray
Perfume
Artificially scented soap, shampoo, moisturizer, deodorant etc.

Pest control
Wood preservative
Garden sprays
Fly spray

Heating
Fumes from gas boilers, kerosene, oil stoves.
Free standing butane or propane heaters are very bad.

Decorating
Paint stripper
Paint and varnish
Fungicide in wallpaper paste
Turpentine, white spirit

Motor vehicles
Gases from upholstery
Petrol or diesel fumes
Evaporating oil from engines
Exhaust fumes from garages under living quarters

Miscellaneous
Dry cleaning fumes (air clothes outdoors after cleaning)
Tobacco smoke
Drugs and medicines
Mould (mold) spores from damp surroundings or damp cloths
Dust
Gases released by new carpets and furnishings, foam rubber, mattresses
Fumes from gas cookers
Newsprint (open newspapers outdoors before bringing in to read)
Creosote
Butane in spray cans
Surgical spirit
Glue

4. Superfoods

Once upon a time we had to take it on trust that so-called 'superfoods' could actually help our health. Naturopathy books used old-fashioned terms such as 'blood cleansing and purifying', 'blood building' and 'strengthening the body'.

Now research has shown us that superfoods really do have amazing health-building properties. And we now know *how* these foods work.

For instance we now know that the 'blood building' properties of beetroot refer to its rich iron content. We know that the 'detoxifying' effects of broccoli and cabbage refer to their sulphur compounds, which help to make enzymes involved in liver detoxification. We know that the 'cleansing' effect of celery refers to its coumarin content, which helps macrophages break down unwanted debris. The so-called 'circulation strengthening' effects of blue and purple berries refers to their role in the integrity of capillary walls and so helping to prevent water retention.

In fact, the more our scientific knowledge grows about the human body, the more it is verifying what the early naturopaths tried to teach us.

The following superfoods are extremely protective of our health and are recommended for regular consumption.

Beets

Beetroot contains a deep red pigment called betanin. This is *not* the same as betaine, with which it is sometimes confused. Most dietary betaine comes from bread and cereals.

In the 1950s, Hungarian physician Dr Alexander Ferenczi became known for his treatments consisting of feeding grated beetroot and 1 litre of diluted beetroot juice daily to cancer patients. He documented what he believed were many cures of cancer which he attributed to this treatment. However other holistic doctors, including the renowned herbalist Rudolf Fritz Weiss MD who attended his presentations could not get the same results. They also pointed out that Ferenczi's 'before and after' X-rays were not supported by tissue specimens, therefore the shadows on these X-rays could just have been areas of inflammation, not tumours.

Recent research suggests that beets have powerful antioxidant properties. Beetroot is considered to be among the ten most potent antioxidant vegetables. It is also a good source of iron.

In 2016 the American College of Cardiology conducted a study demonstrating that exercise capacity improved by 24 per cent after older patients suffering from heart failure were given daily doses of beetroot juice for just one week.

Please be aware that beetroot juice stains the urine and stools red.

Blue and purple fruits

These fruits are rich in pigments known as anthocyanins (literally means 'blue flower'). Anthocyanins are powerful antioxidants which come under the general category of flavonoids. They are found in blueberries, cranberries, bilberries, red and black raspberries, blackberries, blackcurrants, elderberries (very potent source), cherries, eggplant peel, black rice, black grapes, red cabbage and naturally-ripened black olives. Some vegetables, such as potatoes and broccoli, cabbage, cauliflower, carrots, tomatoes and corn, are now being bred to have blue or purple flesh, so these foods may also become a source of anthocyanins.

One of the best sources of anthocyanins is the seed coat of black soybeans. Some rainforest berries are particularly good sources. The Amazonian açaí berry contains about 320 mg of anthocyanin per 100 grams of powdered fruit, but the Patagonian maqui berry is the world's most potent source of anthocyanins, yielding 4000-5000 mg per 100 grams of powdered fruit. Supplements made from these powders are often sold as weight loss aids, but I have not been able to find any research to verify whether they really work in this way.

Like other flavonoids, anthocyanins are valuable in the human body, not just as powerful antioxidants, but also in maintaining the integrity of small blood vessels. This is particularly important for the eyes. A flavonoid deficiency can cause blood capillaries to leak fluid and protein. When this happens in the eyes, damage can occur, in time leading to blindness.

Cayenne (chillies)

Medical herbalists regard chillies as useful to stimulate the adrenal glands, the circulation and the digestion, especially in debilitated people and the elderly. Like many other spices, chillies are also very good to help prevent intestinal gas.

Blood sugar control

A recent interesting clinical trial suggests that the habitual consumption of chillies may be useful to help prevent excessive rises in insulin after a meal. This research has great significance since excessive insulin in the blood is not only a sign of insulin resistance—a condition which precedes type II diabetes—but also prevents dieters from losing body fat.

Cancers

Like ginger and turmeric (see below), chillies also inhibit the production of NF-kappa-B, a protein which cancerous tumours use to help themselves continue growing.

Celery

Celery juice is easy to make, is rich in minerals and has two special benefits.

Firstly it helps to alkalinize the body, which is helpful for general health as well as helping to prevent and alleviate allergic symptoms and the effects of consuming too much protein.

Secondly celery juice is a rich source of a natural substance known as coumarin, which helps macrophages break down unwanted protein deposits. This effect, together with its mild diuretic action, makes celery juice a very good remedy to treat water retention and related conditions. For instance a daily glass of celery juice can be an effective treatment for arthritis caused by inflammatory fluid pressure on joints. Supplements of celery seed extract can also work in a similar way.

Like broccoli, celery is able to induce liver detoxification enzymes.

Celery juice can be diluted with water or mixed with apple, cucumber, tomato or lemon juice or other flavourings.

Celery seed oil is an effective mosquito repellant. In tests it was found to be more potent than the chemical product DEET.

Cinnamon

Cinnamon has long been used by medical herbalists for its anti-microbial, anti-parasitic, digestive stimulant and intestinal gas-relieving properties. In traditional Chinese medicine cinnamon is highly regarded as an aid to weight loss by warming the body (stimulating the metabolism) and so driving off water retention.

Alzheimer's disease

Recent animal tests suggest that cinnamon may help to prevent and even reverse Alzheimer's disease (AD). Cinnamon inhibits the formation of the toxic proteins which are associated with the development of AD. When given as a treatment to mice with AD, cinnamon also improve cognitive behaviour.

Water retention

Cinnamon tea is a good source of coumarin and so (like celery juice) is helpful in fighting some types of water retention.

Anti-diabetic

A number of researchers are becoming interested in cinnamon's anti-diabetic action. Of all the herbs and spices, cinnamon is thought to be the most useful in this regard.

Blood pressure

Research has found that a dose of 2 grams a day of cinnamon can help to reduce high blood pressure.

Cancer

Like turmeric, ginger and chillies, cinnamon also inhibits the activity of NF-kappa-B, one of the substances which tumours rely on to help them grow.

Helps to balance female hormones

Cinnamon selectively stimulates the adrenal glands to secrete progesterone, so it is very useful for women who have a condition known as 'oestrogen dominance'.

Coconut oil

Coconut oil is extracted from the flesh of coconuts and is solid at room temperature. Unlike most other fats and oils, which are primarily made up of long chain triglycerides (LCTs), coconut oil is primarily made up of medium chain triglycerides (MCTs), which makes it very special.

Metabolism

After being eaten, LCTs are transported into the lymphatic system, from where they are deposited in the body's fat layers. On the other hand, MCTs are sent to the liver where they can be turned into energy.

In other words, while most fats are deposited in the body's fat cells, the body burns coconut oil much like carbohydrates for energy. Because of this difference in behaviour, researchers are trying to find out whether MCTs such as coconut oil can aid weight loss by boosting calorie-burning, by faster satiety and causing less fat to be deposited in the body's fat stores. Results so far are encouraging.

So although when you consume coconut oil you get the same satisfaction that you do when you eat fat calories, the net calorie result is less than than fat, because your metabolism rises and you end up burning more of the calories instead of storing them as fat.

Raises HDL, lowers LDL

Research shows that although coconut oil is a saturated fat, it raises HDL (good cholesterol) and lowers LDL (bad cholesterol). It is also capable of reducing abdominal obesity, the type of obesity that causes the harmful 'apple shape'.

Viruses

Infection with the Epstein-Barr virus is said to be one of the potential causes of chronic fatigue syndrome. Coconut oil contains lauric acid, which combats viruses such as Epstein-Barr and others of the herpesvirus family. Coconut oil can be topically applied to the skin as a remedy for herpes but is probably more useful consumed internally.

Intestinal candidiasis

Candidiasis is a fungal infection that commonly arises after taking antibiotics. It causes a wide variety of health problems, from bloating to headaches and severe fatigue. Coconut oil can be useful in preventing candidiasis. It contains caprylic acid, a natural antifungal agent which is also sold in supplement form.

Since the nutritional treatment of candidiasis requires restricting carbohydrate (sugar and starch) consumption, coconut oil can provide a valuable alternative source of dietary energy.

Liver damage

Research carried out on rats given paracetamol (acetaminofen) in doses harmful to the liver, suggests that virgin coconut oil has a protective effect against liver damage caused by toxins.

Thyroid

Some individuals claim that coconut oil can reverse hypothyroidism, but there is as yet no research at all to confirm this. It may eventually be confirmed, but in our view the arguments given to support this view are too flawed to take it too seriously just yet.

Coriander leaf (cilantro)

Coriander leaves have been traditionally used as an anti-diabetic herb.

Heavy metals and viruses

Coriander leaf is used to accelerate the excretion of the heavy metals mercury, lead and aluminium. One researcher believes that viral infections like herpes simplex and cytomegalovirus can only be eliminated for good when coriander leaf is used together with other treatments. He theorizes that perhaps viruses are more easily able to hide and flourish in areas with concentrations of heavy metals.

Alzheimer's disease

In animal studies coriander leaf has been shown to improve memory so it may help to reverse Alzheimer's disease.

Liver protector

Coriander leaf has a protective effect on the liver when tested against damage from carbon tetrachloride.

Coriander seeds

According to *Bartram's Encylopedia of Herbal Medicine*, coriander seeds are a traditional Chinese remedy for measles.

Cruciferous vegetables

The cruciferous (or brassica) family of vegetables includes broccoli, cabbage, cauliflower, Brussels sprouts, kale, radishes and turnips. These vegetables are extremely good at helping to prevent cancer due to some sulphur compounds they contain: sulforaphane and indoles.

Sulforaphane is a potent inducer of the important antioxidant glutathione and also induces the production of enzymes that can deactivate free radicals and carcinogens. Both sulforaphanes and indoles stimulate the production of liver detoxification enzymes. Indoles are particularly good at helping the liver break down excess oestradiol—a potent form of oestrogen. Since a high proportion of breast cancer cases, as well as most endometriosis, fibroids, cystic breast disease and ovarian cysts is caused by excessively high levels of oestradiol, women in particular should cultivate the habit of consuming cruciferous vegetables as often as possible. Broccoli, savoy cabbage, and particularly Brussels sprouts (20-50 times more potent than broccoli) have the most powerful anti-cancer effect.

Garlic

Numerous research studies have confirmed the anti-bacterial, anti-parasitic, anti blood-clotting, cholesterol-lowering, blood fats-lowering and blood-pressure lowering effects of garlic. Some research has found that garlic improves the ability of the pancreas to produce insulin. Some components of garlic may also inhibit the growth of cancerous cells.

Garlic contains a substance known as alliin. When garlic is chopped or crushed, alliin comes into contact with the enzyme allinase, to produce the odorous and medicinally active substance allicin. Allicin is unstable and is lost when garlic is cooked, distilled or chopped and left to stand for a few days. Without allicin, garlic loses its anti-microbial properties, although some experts believe that it may still retain some of its other effects. Others disagree. According to the late renowned German herbalist Rudolph Fritz Weiss MD, if the smell is reduced, so is the medicinal action.

Allicin, the active principle in garlic, enters the bloodstream when ingested, soon reaching all parts of the body. Elimination is mainly via the lungs and skin, which is why the breath and sweat have the characteristic smell of garlic. As it pervades the lungs, garlic sterilizes the alveoli and bronchial tree of the lungs and loosens phlegm, so is helpful against bronchial infections. It also has expectorant properties, and is sometimes added to cough medications.

Infections

Garlic has been used effectively to treat dysentery, typhoid, cholera, bacterial food poisoning, and worm infestations. Weiss describes it as particularly useful after amoebic dysentery when the bowels are still irritable, finding that it helps to heal the bowel with its significantly antibacterial, antispasmodic digestive soothing properties.

Unlike antibiotics, bacteria do not seem to become resistant to garlic. Garlic extract has been found effective against the MRSA 'superbug'.

Aids

One of the most exciting recent studies in garlic research is that reported at a 1989 Aids conference. Ten HIV-positive patients with severely low natural killer cell activity, abnormal helper-to-suppressor T-cell ratios (both these parameters are indicators of advanced Aids, probably with short life expectancy) and opportunistic infections such as cryptosporidial diarrhoea were given 5 grams daily for six weeks and then 10 grams daily for six weeks of a garlic extract. Three patients died before the trial ended, but seven of the 10 experienced a return to normal natural killer cell activity by the end of the 12 weeks. Chronic diarrhoea and candidiasis also improved. (*Int Conf AIDS [Canada] 5:466, 1989. ISBN 0-662-56670-X*). Various trials have shown garlic to be effective against cryptococcus, cryptosporidia, herpes, mycobacteria and pneumocystis—all common infectious agents in Aids.

A good way to take fresh garlic is nightly consumption of a raw garlic clove cut into small cubes with a sharp knife and swallowed with a small glass of water. This results in minimal odour. It can also help to prevent diarrhoea-type infections when travelling in developing countries.

Ginger

Ginger has antioxidant, anti-inflammatory and anti-cancer properties, and can contribute to the treatment of arthritis.

Digestion

In Traditional Chinese Medicine, ginger (like black pepper, garlic and chilli) is classed as a pungent food with warming, outward-moving properties. This is very similar to saying that it is a circulation stimulant and vasodilator. These properties help bring the blood to the surface in the digestive system, thus warming the digestion and improving the production of digestive juices and the absorption of nutrients from the digestive tract into the blood.

For individuals suffering from poor digestion, drinking a cup of strong ginger tea 15 minutes before a meal can help to stimulate gastric juice production.

Pain relief

Clinical trials have shown that the daily consumption of ginger can significantly reduce muscle pain following exercise. Ginger can also provide pain relief when applied as a compress on joints affected by osteoarthritis. These findings may be partly explained by ginger's action as a circulatory stimulant.

Nausea

Ginger is an effective remedy to reduce travel sickness as well as the 'morning sickness' of pregnancy.

Cancer

Although not as extensively researched as turmeric (*see below*), ginger seems to have a similar inhibitory effect on the growth of cancer cells.

Green tea

The flavonoids in green tea are known as polyphenols. Ninety per cent of tea polyphenols are in a form known as catechins. Catechins are what make green tea special. They make up the bulk of green tea's antioxidants, and therefore its healing potential. When black tea is made, catechins oxidize to form more complex compounds which have less antioxidant potential.

Green tea contains six types of catechins. Epigallo-catechin gallate (EGCG) is thought to be the most potent. About half of the catechin content of tea is EGCG. EGCG is found in no other plant than tea, and is one of the most potent antioxidants yet discovered. EGCG is the focus of almost every scientific study involving green tea, and has been associated with most of the newly discovered green tea benefits

Just a small quantity of tea leaves will steep many cups of tea. It is this relative abundance that makes green tea special. One gram of green tea steeped for 3-5 minutes in 100 millimeters of water yields 127 milligrams of catechins. In comparison, 100 grams of dark chocolate contains 54 milligrams of antioxidants, blueberries 52 milligrams and black grapes only 22 milligrams.

The level of EGCG present in tea leaves is highest in young tea buds. These tender sprouts are reserved for making the highest grade tea.

Anti-diabetic

Research carried out at the U.S. Department of Agriculture reveals that EGCG potentiates insulin. This means the body needs to produce less insulin to do the same job, so there is less risk of getting metabolic syndrome—the prediabetic condition caused by high insulin levels. The beneficial effect is lost when milk is added.

Cancers

Like a number of other superfood ingredients, EGCG can fight cancers by suppressing the proliferation of cancer cells and helping to cut off the blood supply to cancers.

In one study, animals with bone cancer showed a dramatic reduction in tumour size after 24 days of treatment with EGCG. EGCG caused cancer cell death by inhibiting the cancer cells' ability to produce energy.

Genital warts

Green tea catechins are a useful treatment for external anogenital warts.

Weight loss

Green tea is thought to help with weight loss by speeding up the burning of calories, fat oxidation, and maintaining the metabolic rate during weight loss. Extracts of EGCG are now found in many popular 'fat burner' supplements.

Cardiovascular disease

Drinking green tea helps to prevent death from strokes and heart attacks.

Leafy green vegetables

These vegetables include dark green cabbage, kale, spinach, rocket (arugula), watercress and spring (collard) greens. Their importance as a daily component of the diet cannot be over-emphasized. Leafy greens are one of the few sources of lutein and zeaxanthins, carotenoids that are selectively taken up into the macula of the eye, where they protect against the development of age-related macular degeneration—a leading cause of blindness.

Leafy greens are one of the few good dietary sources of magnesium and folic acid. They are also good sources of iron and vitamins C and K.

Calcium from kale is better absorbed by the body than calcium from milk.

Radishes

Like chillies, garlic, mustard and ginger, radishes are classed as pungent in traditional Chinese medicine. All these foods are good for helping to soften and loosen phlegm. Radish juice is particularly suitable so is a good treatment for coughs and the common cold.

The long white 'mooli' or 'daikon' radishes are ideal for juicing, but any type of radish can be juiced. Leave the juice to stand for 20 minutes before drinking, since freshly-made radish juice is extremely pungent. Only a small amount is needed. This juice can be mixed with other juices such as apple or carrot.

Thyroid

Due to the publication of *Heinerman's Encyclopedia of Healing Juices*, you will now see references everywhere on the internet to the use of radish juice as a treatment for both an underactive and overactive thyroid. John Heinerman was told by Russian doctors that radishes contain a sulphur compound known as raphanin, which regulates thyroxine production by the thyroid gland.

We have not been able to verify that radish juice helps an underactive thyroid, but radishes belong to the cruciferous vegetable family, and have a similar anti-iodine action as the other members of the family when they are consumed in raw form. So it may be advisable to consume iodine-rich foods such as seafood and seaweed if you are concerned about iodine depletion when consuming raw cruciferous vegetables or their juices.

On the other hand there are some suggestions that radish juice would seem to be a useful treatment for an overactive thyroid.

Digestion

Radish juice is traditionally used as a tonic for the digestive system and gall-bladder, and is especially good for constipation. It does not stimulate bile production but its tonic effect may allow bile to flow more easily when there is congestion.

Cancer

Researchers are recently becoming interested in radishes for their ability to prevent cancer and promote cancer cell death.

Soy

Tofu has been traditionally fed to babies in Japan for hundreds of years, but not in large amounts. Any concentrated commercial forms of soy are definitely not a superfood. They have caused cases of abnormal development when fed to young birds or animals. The thyroid gland is particularly vulnerable to damage from concentrated soy products. A retrospective epidemiological study showed that, when compared to healthy siblings or control group children, teenage children with a diagnosis of autoimmune thyroid disease were more likely to have received soy formula as infants.

Contrary to some of the anti-soy writings on the internet, soy does not contain 'plant oestrogens' (estrogens) but oestrogen modulators or balancers. Oestrogens are known to stimulate the growth of some types of breast cancer, whereas research shows that soy has the opposite effect. For adult women, soy reduces excessive oestrogen levels by binding to oestrogen receptors, and can also raise oestrogen to more normal levels if it is low.

Current findings in soy research

- A daily consumption of natural soy foods can help to prevent the gain in abdominal fat which occurs in post-menopausal women.
- Soy has a significantly protective effect against breast cancer.
- Soy helps maintain bone mineral density
- Soy foods help to prevent colon cancer. This may be because soy up-regulates enzymes which help convert vitamin D to its active form.

We do not recommend that you eat soy-based 'meat substitutes' or take soy isoflavone supplements. These are highly concentrated forms of soy which have been known to interfere with thyroid gland function.

Consuming the amounts of soy found in traditional Asian diets has not been shown to be harmful. Natural soy products include soy flour, tofu, soy milk, tempeh and soy yoghurt.

Genetic modification

Unless a soy product is labelled as organic, it is likely to be contaminated with genetically-modified soybeans, which are now widely prevalent.

Turmeric

Turmeric contains a powerful yellow pigment called curcumin. Curcumin is non-toxic and can be safely taken in supplement form. It is not well absorbed if taken alone, but absorption can be improved by dissolving it in hot water or warm oils together with black pepper. We recommend adding as much turmeric as possible to hot lentil and vegetable soup, plus black pepper and olive oil and any other ingredients that help the soup's flavour.

The liver

Curcumin is one of the most powerful of all antioxidants and has wide-ranging beneficial effects, particularly for the liver. It is by far the best natural treatment for liver inflammation (hepatitis) and also assists liver drainage and repair. Consuming turmeric is one of the few ways of naturally increasing glutathione levels in the body.

Turmeric is particularly good for people with chemical sensitivity caused by an imbalance in the phases of liver detoxification.

Anti-inflammatory action

Curcumin can help to treat osteoarthritis by protecting cartilage from being damaged by inflammatory reactions in the body.

Curcumin's potent anti-inflammatory action makes it an important part of natural treatments for auto-immune disorders.

Some researchers consider obesity to be an inflammatory condition, and see turmeric as a useful aid to treat some of the biological causes of obesity.

Cancers

Curcumin is one of the most potent known anti-carcinogenic (cancer prevention) substances. Its antioxidant and free radical quenching properties, including the ability to scavenge DNA-damaging superoxide radicals, allow it to significantly protect the body against exposure to carcinogenic chemicals and pollutants.

But the most exciting recent developments in curcumin research relate to its role in the *treatment* of cancer.

Apart from vitamin C megadoses, there are few natural substances known to have a direct anti-cancer effect. Most work only indirectly, by fighting free radicals and providing optimum nutritional support for the immune system.

Turmeric is different, and many researchers are now excited about its treatment potential. There are several ways in which turmeric can help to treat cancers:

Anti-angiogenic

Angiogenesis is the process whereby new blood vessels grow which supply and nourish the tumour. Angiogenesis is essential for tumour growth and spread. Curcumin from turmeric has been shown to have an anti-angiogenic effect in animal studies using grafts of various tumours.

Anti-metastatic

Metastasis is the process whereby tumours produce 'seed' cells which migrate to other parts of the body and invade them to form secondary tumours. Few people with secondaries have been known to survive for long.

Curcumin's anti-metastatic effect has been demonstrated in animal studies on breast cancer, resulting in suppressed cell migration and invasion.

Curcumin's therapeutic effects against cancer are thought to be due to its ability to suppress NF-κB, a gene regulator which tumours use to help them spread.

Researchers are becoming interested in using curcumin as an adjunctive treatment for radio– and chemotherapy.

Case study

In 2002 we advised a client who was undergoing chemotherapy for breast cancer, to consume daily broccoli and as much turmeric as possible to help protect her liver from the effects of the toxic drugs. She managed to consume at least a teaspoon a day of turmeric. After two months she reported that her tumour had shrunk to the size of a small pea and that this was a great surprise to her doctors (who were never told that she had been taking dietary advice).

Part II
Getting organized

1. Shopping and saving time

If you are using this book to try to overcome any kind of health problem, you'll need to be well-organized from the start. Most people fail at a special diet because they arrive home tired and hungry, open the fridge and find nothing compatible with the diet. 'Oh blow it!' they say, 'I'll eat this packet of biscuits / cookies and go back on the diet tomorrow.' Needless to say, tomorrow may never come.

Most of us want to spend the absolute minimum of time shopping and in the kitchen. As I heard someone say recently 'I thought cooking was making toast and reading the instructions on the microwave packet'. I love good food, but I too find it hard to spend hours making intricate meals. All the recipes in this book reflect that because I use them myself.

Before you get cooking, let's look at some of the ingredients you should always have in your fridge or store-cupboard (see panel on right). If you make sure you don't run out, you will always be able to whip up a delicious meal in minutes. And it's guaranteed to be a lot cheaper than a shop-bought ready meal.

Most of these foods can now be bought in the larger supermarkets as well as in health food stores.

**Meals in Minutes
Shopping List**

Apples
Beans, dried or canned in plain water
Blueberry or black cherry all-fruit jam
Brown rice
Canned plum tomatoes
Carrots
Dried fruit
Filleted fish for freezing
Frozen chopped mixed vegetables
Garlic
Gluten-free flour
Green cabbage
Herbs and spices
Lemons or limes
Lentils
Low-sodium salt
Nuts (almonds, cashews, walnuts, brazils, unsalted peanuts)
Oatflakes
Olive oil (extra-virgin)
Onions
Potatoes, especially Desirée or other waxy varieties
Prawns (shrimps)
Pumpernickel bread (long-life, yeast– and wheat-free)
Rice noodles
Sunflower seeds
Sweet (bell) peppers
Tamari sauce
Tofu
Tomato purée (paste)

Equipment

If you would like to take advantage of the recipes which use ingredients that you prepare in advance and then freeze to make quick meals later on, a freezer would be a great advantage. And, since one of the best-value sources of protein is the humble dried bean or pea, I am also recommending that you obtain a pressure-cooker. I gave up years ago trying to cook beans, split peas and so on in a normal saucepan. Two hours after starting to boil them they can still be like bullets! In a pressure cooker, even the toughest bean will yield to pressure in 5-10 minutes and become deliciously tender.

Canned beans in plain water (e.g. kidney, pinto or borlotti beans) can be a good stand-by, but not only do they cost more than dried beans, they are often quite hard and chewy, and not always pleasant to eat.

I also like to use a wok or stir-fry pan (preferably with a see-through lid) for a lot of recipes, but if you cook with electricity, you should substitute a frying pan with deep sides or a sauté pan. Another useful piece of equipment is a food processor. If you get one with a vegetable juicing attachment, you will be able to make some of the therapeutic juices mentioned in this book

Cooking brown rice

Frozen rice and beans are a great standby. You can make a lot of really delicious fast recipes by combining these in different ways. You could also use canned beans but they are more expensive and may be loaded with salt and sugar.

Brown rice is nuttier than white rice, with a different texture. It contains all the B vitamins that are lost when rice is 'polished'. You can buy brown rice from supermarkets and health food stores.

To cook brown rice, wash well, then pre-soak overnight in twice its volume of water. Use the same water for cooking. Bring to the boil then cover tightly and simmer on the lowest possible heat until tender (20-25 minutes). Don't worry if you haven't soaked it before cooking, you can also cook it without prior soaking, though I think that soaking gives it a nicer texture.

When cooked, drain away any remaining excess water then leave the rice in the covered saucepan away from the heat for five minutes, after which it is ready to serve.

Once cold, brown rice can be spread out on an oiled baking tray, frozen, then crumbled into grains and bagged for the freezer.

Cooking dried beans

These must be soaked in water before use. Cover with at least four times their volume in boiling water and leave overnight.

Throw away the soaking water, place the beans, well covered with fresh water, in a pressure cooker, bring to full steam, and leave on a low-medium heat for 3-10 minutes, depending on size and age. You may need to experiment a few times to get it right. I have a Tower stainless steel pressure cooker, and give borlotti and pinto beans 10 minutes, but your pressure cooker may vary.

Remove from the heat and leave to cool or place the pressure cooker in a sink of cold water. You cannot open the pressure cooker until it has cooled down enough to reduce the steam pressure inside. Do not try!

Remove the lid and bite a bean to ensure that it is tender. If not, return the beans to the pan and cook for a little longer.

Pressure-cooking breaks down the poisonous lectins found in raw beans. If you do not have a pressure cooker, boil them fast for at least 10 minutes after soaking and before simmering or slow-cooking.

To freeze, allow the beans to cool and follow the same method as for frozen brown rice. Spoonfuls of any pulses (legumes) which end up a little mushy can be frozen in the wells of tart or muffin baking tins before bagging.

Cooking lentils

Lentils are so easy to cook, and once frozen they can be used to make a substantial one-pot meal in ten minutes.

Use half a cup / 115 ml uncooked lentils per serving. Put the lentils in a large pan and add about 2½ times their volume of boiling water plus a tablespoon of olive oil to stop them frothing up too much.

Never add salt at this stage, as it will toughen them. Bring to the boil and simmer for 25-40 minutes, depending on the size and age of the lentils. Stir occasionally and add more boiling water if they seem to be drying out. Red lentils take only 25 minutes. Brown, green or yellow lentils take 30 to 40 minutes. Lentils boil over easily, which is why it is a good idea to use a pan several sizes larger than you would normally need.

To freeze cooked lentils, allow them to cool and put spoonfuls in the wells of tart or muffin baking tins. Freeze the tins then empty out the frozen lentils, put them in bags and return to the freezer.

2. Cooking techniques

Maximizing nutrients

I can't help cringing when I visit someone's kitchen and watch a few handfuls of chopped vegetables rapidly boiling in a huge panful of water.

One of the first rules of cookery is that most of the vitamins from vegetables end up in the cooking water. So the second rule is to use only a small amount of cooking water and keep it to make soup, sauce or gravy; or use a cooking method which doesn't need any water. Here are some alternatives to boiling.

Steaming

This is a good method for potatoes, since only an inch of water is needed in the bottom of the pan. You don't need to buy a special steamer. Cheap metal steaming baskets are available which open up to fit inside any saucepan. You may need to allow the potatoes a few extra minutes' cooking time, and do ensure that the water is kept boiling quite briskly.

Potato water contains vitamin C and can be saved (or frozen) for adding to soup. In continental Europe some doctors recommend drinking potato water to help soothe bowel spasms in irritable bowel syndrome. This is because potatoes are related to Belladonna and contain small amounts of atropine-like compounds.

Braising and sautées

Braising is a wonderful way to cook vegetables. You just stir vegetable pieces (add chopped onion for extra succulence) into a little oil over a medium heat, and then add just a few tablespoons of water. After bringing the liquid to the boil, cover the pan very tightly and turn the heat down to the lowest possible setting. Check every five minutes and add a little more water if the vegetables are getting too dry. The vegetables cook very slowly in their own juices. The result? Delicious!

Sautées are similar but you add more liquid. Once the food is cooked you remove it, reduce the sauce by boiling, and then pour the sauce back over the food.

Stir-frying

This method is also similar to braising, but the vegetables need to be cut into very small pieces or thin strips, and stirred in a large, roomy pan (preferably a Chinese wok or stir-fry pan) over a high heat until they are part-cooked. A few tablespoons of water are then added to create a lot of steam which helps to soften the vegetables. A lid may then be put over the pan for a short time. Stir-frying is faster than braising. Brown rice can be made delicious by stir-frying in olive oil with some spring onion and garlic. Add chopped herbs, turmeric and a few dashes of tamari sauce.

Soups

Soups are a wonderful way to get all the goodness out of vegetables, since nothing is thrown away. A thick, chunky soup can be a meal in itself, and, as discussed in my soup diet book, it can help you lose weight too.

Baking

If chopped very small (as in a food processor) vegetables can be mixed with chopped nuts and cooked grains such as brown rice or buckwheat, and then tray-baked. Flavoured with herbs, miso or tamari sauce, this deliciously moist dish complements any main item on the menu; or it could be served as a lunchtime snack, on its own or with a sauce.

Refined Foods

Foods made from white flour (e.g. bread, pasta, cookies and cake)

Sugar and syrup of all types

White (polished) rice

Most breakfast cereals

Most cooking oils and margarines.

Foods are refined for various reasons, often to extend their shelf life. Refining means removing part of the food (often the nutrient-rich outer layer) or extracting from the whole food only the part you want (such as sugar or pure oil), leaving up to 90 per cent of the vitamins and minerals behind. The manufacturers may then try to sell you back the wheatgerm or bran removed from the cereals, or the vitamin E extracted from the oils.

By law, refined foods often have to be 'fortified' with added vitamins as they are so depleted. Unrefined foods don't need added vitamins since they can be up to ten times more nutritious.

3. Meals in minutes

Forget burgers, fish sticks, oven fries and canned baked beans—give me fresh potatoes, fresh (or chopped frozen) vegetables, garlic, rice noodles, olive oil, tofu, soy yoghurt and the home-frozen brown rice and beans already mentioned, and I can produce meals in minutes with very little effort. Here are my secrets. All you need are some basic cooking techniques and some herbs and spices for different flavours. Best of all, it's intuitive cooking—you don't even need a recipe. Just make these dishes a couple of times and they will be committed to memory.

Home-made Indian curries

I make a lot of curries, and they are incredibly simple. Here are the basic steps involved. You will need a spice grinder filled with your favourite mixture. I like cloves, cardamom (remove the shells first), black pepper, fennel, coriander seeds and chopped cinnamon pieces. These are good for intestinal health and help prevent gas formation.

1. Heat some oil in a saucepan and add finely chopped onion and garlic. I also like to add some cashew nuts sometimes.
2. When beginning to sizzle gently, grind in some of your spice mixture. Heat for a few seconds until you can smell the aroma.
3. Then for a bean curry just add some of your home-frozen beans. Or you could add cooked lentils instead. For a vegetable curry add any mixture of vegetables:
   - Diced potatoes and shredded cabbage leaves or diced aubergine (eggplant) with coriander (cilantro) leaves
   - Frozen chopped mixed vegetables
   - Cauliflower or broccoli florets, diced courgettes and tomato
   - A packet of ready-prepared 'stir fry' vegetables from the supermarket (ensure no additives).
4. Stir in some powdered turmeric (good for your liver) plus enough water to just cover the ingredients. Stir and season with low-sodium salt. You could also add a spoonful of tomato paste or coconut cream.

5. Simmer gently for about 30 minutes. If there is too much liquid, boil rapidly with the lid off until reduced. Serve with brown rice. I also like to spoon some thick soy or sheep's yoghurt over the top— or see the sour cream recipe on page 205.

Home-made Thai curry

This is even simpler. You will need some Thai curry paste and creamed coconut. Creamed coconut is sold in blocks and is easily available in supermarkets. Thai curry paste ingredients are usually free of major allergens although they may contain a little salt. If you are vegetarian, watch out for brands containing minced shrimps.

You can make this curry with tofu, chicken or fish. The silken variety of tofu is not suitable for this recipe. Ask your health food store for a variety of tofu that is suitable for frying. (In the UK the Cauldron brand is suitable and is available from supermarkets.)

1. If using tofu, cut it into bite-sized chunks, coat with gluten-free flour or rice flour seasoned with cayenne pepper, onion granules and low-sodium salt, and fry in olive oil for about two minutes on each side. Leave to drain on a piece of kitchen paper.
2. Put mixed chopped vegetables in a saucepan, add enough water almost to cover, and bring to a simmer. Stir in Thai curry paste and pieces of coconut cream to taste. Leave to simmer for about 30 minutes then stir in the fried tofu pieces, heat through and serve. If using chicken or fish, add small pieces and simmer gently until cooked through.
3. Serve poured over rice or rice vermicelli. To prepare rice vermicelli simply pour boiling water over it, soak for 2 minutes then drain.

Stir-fried fish with rice noodles

You can use any fish fillets, or frozen peeled shrimps or prawns. You will also need the flat rice noodles which you can buy in Chinese groceries or in larger supermarkets. Cut the fish into bite-sized chunks. Put the chopped frozen vegetables and olive oil in a stir-fry pan. Sprinkle with your choice of dried herbs and some low-sodium salt. Add a few tablespoons of water and cook over a low heat with the lid on for five minutes then add the fish pieces, replace the lid and continue cooking until the fish flakes easily—another five minutes or so.

Meanwhile, soak the noodles for 2-3 minutes in boiling water and drain. If there is any liquid remaining in the stir-fry pan, turn up the heat until it has evaporated. Put the contents of the stir-fry pan in a bowl. Replace the pan on a medium heat, and add another tablespoon of olive oil plus some chopped garlic. When just beginning to sizzle, add the drained noodles and stir-fry over a high heat for half a minute, ensuring that the noodles are coated with oil. Season with low-sodium salt. Then add back the fish and vegetables. Mix well and serve immediately.

Baked potatoes with braised vegetables

While potatoes are baking in the oven, finely chop some onion and add to a stir-fry pan or saucepan with some olive oil over a medium heat. Add the chopped vegetables of your choice: cabbage, carrots, courgettes, green beans, cauliflower florets are all good. Add garlic too if you like it. Cut the vegetables into different shapes to make the mixture more attractive, e.g. carrots into thin strips, French beans left whole, cauliflower florets really small. Stir into the onion, add a few tablespoons of water, and after bringing the water to the boil, cover tightly and cook on the lowest heat setting for 30 minutes. Stir from time to time and check that the vegetables have not dried out. Add a little more water if necessary.

Cut open the baked potatoes and top with the vegetable mixture and a dollop of soy yoghurt (or see the delicious sour cream or garlic crème recipes in Part III).

Vegetable soup

Another great standby is a thick vegetable soup, especially if you are trying to lose weight. Soups fill you up and satisfy you without loading you with calories. Just throw in diced potatoes and every vegetable you can think of. plus a few handfuls of cooked frozen beans, split peas or lentils, a can of organic chopped tomatoes, lots of herbs and garlic and some low-sodium salt. Add enough boiling water to just cover the vegetables, bring the pan to the boil and simmer for about 25 minutes. Thicken the soup by whizzing it with the blender just for 10 seconds or so. You want it to be part blended and part chunky. Finish it off by stirring in a tablespoon of soy cream if you want a cream soup.

A soup made with loads of dark green cabbage or spring greens is an easy and tasty way to eat these vitally important vegetables.

Part III
Gourmet Recipes

Special note

You will find metric, imperial and US cup measurements for the following recipes. Equivalents are never exact, so if you experience any problems, try to use the metric measurements, since these may give more precise results.

I could not find a standard volume for a US cup, so in this book I am making one cup equal to a volume measurement of half a pint.

Before using ingredients that you are not familiar with, it is recommended to look them up in Appendix IV for more information.

Breakfast

Always eat breakfast, even if you are trying to lose weight.

During the night your body slows down its metabolism (burns calories more slowly) to conserve energy. Only when you start eating again does it speed things up.

A carbohydrate-only breakfast will leave you feeling hungry again quite quickly, so make sure you include some protein and oils in your breakfast to keep your blood sugar even. Nuts, fish and avocados are ideal.

Apart from the recipes here, many gluten-free breakfast cereals are now available, and these can be consumed with alternatives to cow's milk, such as nut milks, soy or sheep's milk.

Yoghurt with Almonds and Apple Compote

Makes one serving

Instructions

Swirl 4 tbsp sheep's milk or soy yoghurt into a generous serving of apple sauce (see page 207).

Sprinkle liberally with toasted flaked almonds.

Variations

Apricots or prunes (soaked in water overnight) gently poached until tender also go well with yoghurt.

Sheep's (and cow's) yoghurt has a sharper flavour than soy yoghurt.

For a very filling breakfast, put a cup of sheep's yoghurt in a sieve lined with kitchen paper, and allow to drain into a bowl for one hour. Discard the watery liquid, then put the thickened yoghurt in a dish, and add sliced banana, chopped dates, raisins and crushed walnuts. This is guaranteed to keep you going until lunchtime!

What It's Good For

Both sheep's and soy yoghurts are rich in protein. It's a good idea to start your day with some protein because this is the time of day when your body can best assimilate it.

Protein is also more filling than carbohydrate. An all-carbohydrate breakfast can leave you feeling hungry again within two hours.

Breakfast Corn Pancakes and Waffles

Ingredients to make 4 pancakes

2 heaped tbsp each of

Finely ground yellow polenta meal

Buckwheat flour

Gram (chickpea) or soy flour

(adding up to a combined quantity of about 115 g/4 ounces/½ cup)

250 ml/8½ fluid oz/ generous ¾ cup water

½ tsp baking powder

NB: Waffles use more batter than pancakes.

Instructions

Mix the ingredients well together to form a smooth, runny batter. It should be able to quickly spread to the edges when poured into a pan. Heat a lightly oiled frying pan over a medium to high heat. When hot, pour in enough batter to cover the bottom of the pan and quickly tilt the pan so that the batter can run to the edges, forming a pancake shape. Cook for about one minute, or until small holes form and the top is just set. Turn the pancake over with a spatula (or toss it if you're brave!) and cook the other side for about the same time. Oil the pan again and stir the batter before making the next pancake. Stack the pancakes and keep them warm until you are ready to eat them. Spread with apple butter (see page 207) and cinnamon or ground cardamom, or with all-fruit blueberry jam, and roll them up.

What It's Good For

Yellow polenta flour is rich in anti-cancer carotenes (similar to beta carotene). Buckwheat flour is rich in molybdenum—a mineral needed by the liver for detoxification work. Soy flour is a rich source of hormone-balancing isoflavones which help to prevent problems relating to excess or insufficient oestrogen and excess testosterone. In clinical trials women with menopausal symptoms have reversed them by eating a diet rich in soy flour.

The pancake batter will keep in the fridge for a few days, so you can make just one or two pancakes very quickly. Stir well before cooking.

Waffles

Make a thicker batter, using less water, and spoon it into an oiled, preheated waffle iron. Cook for 2-3 minutes. Turn the waffle upside-down before serving, and spread with pure peanut, cashew or almond butter and/or all-fruit blueberry jam or all-fruit orange marmalade.

Authentic Swiss Muesli with Flaked Nuts and Sweet Apricots

Ingredients for one serving

3 tbsp medium or fine ground gluten-free oatmeal

Water

Soy or almond milk to taste

1 tbsp flaked nuts

1 unsulphured dried apricot, chopped small

Dried apricots are orange in colour if treated with sulphur dioxide. This additive is an intestinal irritant and can cause bloating and gas. Unsulphured apricots (from health food shops) are dark brown and much sweeter in flavour.

Instructions

Did you know that the Swiss never eat muesli straight out of the packet? They know that raw grains should always be soaked (or cooked) before eating them, because this breaks down mildly poisonous chemicals they contain, known as enzyme inhibitors, that can upset your intestines.

Soak the oatmeal overnight in water. The amount of water you need will depend on how much the oatmeal can absorb—about three times its volume for medium oatmeal, and more for fine oatmeal. If you find after an hour or so that the mixture has become too solid, add more water. No milk is necessary since the oats create their own milk. In the morning check the consistency and add a little soy or nut milk if you wish, to achieve your preferred consistency. If you

What It's Good For

Oats and oatmeal are one of the best possible sources of magnesium and B vitamins. These nutrients are often lacking in diets which rely on convenience foods. A magnesium deficiency can reduce your liver's ability to get rid of toxins and can be responsible for many ailments, especially those related to anxiety and stress. Magnesium is rapidly used up in stress situations. Muscles have difficulty relaxing when they are short of magnesium.

use fine oatmeal, the result will be very creamy. Stir in the dried apricot pieces and sprinkle with flaked nuts.

Pure oatmeal is naturally gluten-free, but many oat crops are contaminated with small amounts of wheat or other gluten-containing grains. Oatmeal products which are described as gluten-free do not contain such contaminants.

Fried Herring Cakes

Ingredients for 2 servings

2 medium herrings, scaled, trimmed and gutted

2 tbsp olive oil

2 dessertspoons chickpea (gram) flour

Low-sodium salt

Freshly ground black pepper

Instructions

Poach the herrings in a few tablespoons of water in a lidded pan over a low heat for ten minutes, until the fish comes apart easily. Allow the fish to cool, then slit it open lengthwise and carefully remove all the bones.

Using a fork, mash the fish with the chickpea flour and seasonings, then, using your hands, divide it into four balls and form each ball into a fairly thin patty. Dust the outside of the patties with more chick pea flour.

Heat the oil in a frying pan over a fairly high heat, then put the patties into the pan and fry for 1-2 minutes on each side or until brown. The patties can be prepared the night before for cooking in the morning.

Serve hot with home-made tomato ketchup (see page 204).

What It's Good For

Herrings are rich in omega 3 oils which help prevent heart attacks. They discourage red blood cells from clumping and blocking arteries. If foods were priced according to how healthy they are, few of us would be able to afford herrings. They are probably the best value fish you can get, and very beautiful with shiny, silvery scales. Herrings are also an excellent source of zinc. A zinc deficiency can lead to skin and immunity problems, a poor sense of taste or smell, and to prostate problems in older men.

You could also serve these herring cakes cold as a starter, on a bed of shredded lettuce with lemon wedges. Or tuck them into a gluten-free flatbread and top with salad ingredients and a squeeze of lemon juice.

Sultana and Sunflower Seed Porridge with Milk and Cream

Ingredients for one serving

250 ml/9 fluid oz/generous ¾ cup soy or nut milk

3 tbsp gluten free rolled oats or medium oatmeal

2 tsp raisins

2 tsp sunflower seeds

Soy cream (optional)

Tip

Add a few drops of natural vanilla extract to soy milk to make it taste more like cow's milk. Vanilla is very similar to coumarin, a substance which gives cow's milk its flavour of new-mown hay. Coumarin actually comes from new-mown hay.

Instructions

Put the milk and oats in a small, heavy-bottomed saucepan (enamelled cast iron if you have one) over a medium heat.

Bring to the boil, stirring constantly, then turn down the heat to a simmer and add the raisins and sunflower seeds.

Keep stirring for a minute or two until it thickens. Add a little more milk if you prefer a more runny porridge. Serve with a little soy cream poured over the top.

This is a delicious and satisfying breakfast, especially on a cold winter's day. If you prefer extra sweetness, use a variety of soy milk which has been sweetened with a little apple juice.

This recipe takes only 5 minutes to make.

What It's Good For

Oats are rich in B vitamins, magnesium and dietary fibre. Sunflower seeds are rich in essential polyunsaturated oils, calcium, magnesium and methionine, which is normally not found in large amounts in plant foods. Methionine is turned into glutathione in your liver, which, together with the trace element selenium, makes an important free radical fighting enzyme known as glutathione peroxidase. Unlike animal fats, the omega 6 oils in natural sunflower seeds are very beneficial to health.

Hi-Nutrition Smoothie

Ingredients for 2 servings

One avocado

600 ml/1 pint/2 cups rice milk

One banana, broken into pieces

Half an orange, peeled but with some white outer pith remaining

2 tbsp sheep's yoghurt or thick soy yoghurt or silken tofu

4 Brazil nuts or 2 tbsp ground almonds

Special equipment if using Brazil nuts

Rotary drum grater with handle

Instructions

If using Brazil nuts, wash and dry them, then grate finely using the rotary drum grater. Add the grated Brazils or ground almonds to the rice milk and leave to soak for at least two hours or overnight to improve the digestibility of the nuts.

Open the avocado and remove the stone. Cut the flesh into pieces.

Liquidize all the ingredients together and drink immediately.

Small, ripe avocados with a good flavour are best for this recipe. Liquidized avocado turns brown quickly, so don't let this hang around before drinking it.

What It's Good For

This smoothie can be consumed at any time of day and is ideal for invalids who need a healthy meal replacement formula. The avocado, yoghurt (or tofu) and nuts all provide protein. The avocado and nuts also supply nutritious oils and the vitamin C in the orange helps you to absorb iron from the ingredients. Bananas provide glucose, potassium and vitamin B6. It is well worth using Brazil nuts if you can because they are one of the few good sources of selenium, needed by your liver for detoxification.

Granola

Ingredients for 2 servings

6 tbsp gluten free rolled oats

3 tbsp chopped mixed nuts

2 tbsp sunflower seeds

1 tbsp groundnut oil

1 tbsp raisins

1 tbsp unsulphured dried apricots, diced

A few drops of natural vanilla extract

Instructions

Mix all the ingredients except the dried fruit thoroughly together.

Put a dry frying pan over a low heat. When hot, add the ingredients and cook for 20 minutes, stirring occasionally.

Remove from the heat and stir in the dried fruit. Once cool, store in an airtight container.

To serve, pour into a bowl and add soy or nut milk. You could also add prunes, apple compote or fresh fruit such as bananas, pears or strawberries.

What It's Good For

This delicious, nutty cereal can be eaten for breakfast or as a snack at any time of day. See page 66 for the benefits of oats and sunflower seeds. Dried fruit is rich in the mineral potassium. Groundnut oil has been used in this recipe because it has to be heated. Like olive oil, groundnut oil contains mainly monounsaturated fatty acids, which are less easily damaged by heat than most other oils. Groundnut oil also has little flavour of its own, and so is ideal for recipes like this.

Avocado Smoothie with Banana and Strawberries

Ingredients for 2 servings

One avocado

600 ml/1 pint/2 cups soy milk

Half a banana, broken into pieces

One handful of sweet strawberries

1 tsp natural vanilla extract

Instructions

Probably the fastest breakfast in the universe!

Open the avocado and remove the stone. Cut the flesh into pieces.

Liquidize all the ingredients together and drink immediately.

Small, ripe avocados with a good flavour are best for this recipe. Liquidized avocado turns brown quickly, so don't let this hang around before drinking it.

What It's Good For

Described as one of nature's most perfect foods, creamy, buttery avocados are so nutritious that they are practically a whole meal in themselves. They are rich in protein, omega 6 polyunsaturated oils, vitamin B6 and other B vitamins, vitamin E, iron and copper, and provide three times as much potassium as bananas. They are also easy to digest. The rough-skinned Hass avocado has a particularly good flavour. The protein in this drink will help to keep you going until lunchtime.

Lunches, suppers snacks & starters

A really cool way to serve a family meal or a dinner for guests is to make it a sit-down tapas-style meal where people help themselves from a variety of hot or cold dishes.

Try arranging a selection of the following dishes in the centre of the dining table:

- ◊ Eggplant Caviar
- ◊ Frittata with Ginger and Courgettes
- ◊ Potato Wedges Roasted with Olive Oil and Garlic
- ◊ Guacamole
- ◊ Falafel
- ◊ Mini Rainbow Salads
- ◊ German Potato Salad
- ◊ Pumpernickel, and rye crispbread.

Or put out the ingredients for Danish Open Sandwiches and let people build their own.

And of course buffets are great for parties and the cold items for packed lunches too.

Russian Borscht

Ingredients for 6-8 servings

1.7 litres/3 pints/6 cups water

¼ head small to medium green cabbage, coarsely shredded

2 medium potatoes, cut into four lengthwise, then thinly sliced

3 medium beetroot (beets), boiled whole, peeled, cooled and coarsely grated

2 medium carrots, coarsely grated

1 medium onion

1 small can tomato purée (paste)

4 cloves garlic, peeled

2 tbsp extra virgin olive oil

Low-sodium salt

Instructions

Put the potatoes and shredded cabbage in a large saucepan with the water and low-sodium salt and bring to the boil. Simmer for 15 minutes then add the grated carrot and simmer for a further 5 minutes.

Meanwhile cut the onion into 8 pieces and process with the garlic cloves in a food processor with the S blade.

Heat the oil in a stir-fry pan or sauté pan, and stir the onion and garlic mixture over a medium heat until softened but not brown.

When the cabbage, potato and carrot are tender, stir in the tomato purée then add the softened onion and garlic mixture, followed by the grated beetroot. Gently heat through until just simmering, then serve in bowls topped with a dollop of sour cream (see page 205).

What It's Good For

Beetroot is a wonderful herb-like food which stimulates your liver cells and is one of the richest plant sources of iron in a well-assimilated form. Cabbage is a great anti-cancer vegetable, since it helps your liver to process toxins into more harmless substances. It is also rich in a powerful antioxidant flavonoid known as quercetin which has been found to help prevent cataracts and allergic problems. Use the darkest green cabbage you can find.

Eggplant Caviar

Ingredients for 2-4 servings

1 medium eggplant (aubergine), washed and dried

1 small onion, finely chopped in a food processor

2 medium tomatoes, skinned, deseeded and roughly chopped

2 tbsp lemon juice

Extra virgin olive oil

1 tbsp parsley, finely chopped

Low-sodium salt

Black pepper

Parsley or coriander leaf (cilantro) to garnish

Instructions

Steam the eggplant whole (or cut in half to fit the pan) for 15 minutes until soft. Sweat the onion over a medium heat for 5 minutes with 2 tbsp olive oil. When the eggplant is ready, dice it finely and add it to the pan with the onions. Stir, cover the pan and continue cooking very gently for another 5 minutes, then turn off the heat. Stir in the chopped tomatoes, parsley, low-sodium salt and pepper, lemon juice and another tablespoon of olive oil. Mix and incorporate thoroughly. Allow to cool, then chill and garnish with a sprig of parsley or coriander (cilantro) before serving on a bed of shredded iceberg lettuce. Serve as part of a buffet meal or put teaspoonfuls on cucumber slices or mini-poppadoms, or flatbreads or small squares of wheat- and yeast-free pumpernickel and top with a dollop of sour cream (see page 205).

What It's Good For

Russians really do eat this dish, and call it caviar. Many prefer it to the real thing. In Ayurvedic medicine eggplant is considered a potent food to support a woman's hormonal processes. Aubergines are known as eggplants because of their creamy texture when cooked. They do not contain 'bitter juices' and do not need to be treated with salt before cooking. If you throw away their juice you will throw away a lot of their nutritional value.

This dish is better if made the day before and kept cool before serving.

Variation

Can also be made with raw onion or spring onion (scallion) instead of cooked.

Bean Burgers

Ingredients for 2 servings

2 large handfuls of soft cooked borlotti beans

1 large handful of grated potato

2 tbsp finely chopped shallots or spring onions (scallions)

1 clove garlic, finely chopped

Few tbsp olive oil

Low-sodium salt

Freshly-ground black pepper

Special equipment

A baking tray with six shallow, round, burger-shaped wells. Oil the wells before use so that the burgers can be removed easily after freezing.

Instructions

Squeeze as much water out of the grated potato as you can. It should be as dry as possible.

Gently fry the chopped shallots and garlic in a pan with the olive oil until softened. Add the beans, stir until heated through then crush them with a potato masher in the frying pan. Add the grated potato and seasoning and incorporate thoroughly. Fry for 3 minutes, turning and stirring so that the mixture cooks evenly.

Remove from the heat and spoon the mixture into the oiled wells of the baking tray. Place the tray in the freezer. Once frozen the burgers can be removed from the tray and bagged.

Cook the burgers from frozen. Fry in a hot pan for 2 minutes on each side or until heated through, crisp and golden. Serve with green salad and a potato or vegetable dish. You can used canned beans for this recipe, but beans you have cooked as described on page 48 will have a better texture. Frozen beans are fine—you can add them straight to the frying pan.

What It's Good For

Beans are a good source of protein, zinc, B vitamins and soluble fibre. This kind of fibre helps you keep feeling full for longer as it is very beneficial for keeping your blood sugar in balance.

Detoxification Soup

Ingredients for 6 servings

1.7 litres/3 pints/6 cups water
225 g/½ lb white fish, cut into chunks
1 long, white (mooli/daikon) radish, cut into matchsticks
1 medium onion, chopped
2 boiled, peeled beetroot (beets), diced
225 g/½ lb brussels sprouts, sliced
1 small can of tomato purée (paste)
2 tbsp extra virgin olive oil
1 tbsp gelatine
2 tsp turmeric (yellow oriental spice)
Low-sodium salt

Instructions

Sweat the chopped onion gently in the olive oil, in the bottom of a large saucepan. When softened, stir in the turmeric until it is thoroughly incorporated. Pour in the water and bring almost to the boil. When nearly boiling, remove from the heat, sprinkle in the gelatine powder and whisk until dissolved, then stir in the tomato purée. Finally, add the fish and vegetables, except the beetroot. Season with low-sodium salt.

Bring back to the boil and simmer gently for 20 minutes. Gently stir in the diced beetroot and serve.

What It's Good For

This recipe is medicinal, with four sets of ingredients to help your liver (i) **Clear toxins from your blood** (brussels sprouts, beets, protein, glycine (gelatine); (ii) **Neutralize toxic free radicals produced in your liver:** (quercetin (onions), vitamin C (brussels sprouts), lycopene (tomato purée); (iii) **Help the flow of bile to flush wastes from liver and gallbladder into intestines and stools** (radish, turmeric); (iv) **Help protect your liver cells against toxic damage** (turmeric).

Frittata (Italian Omelette) with Ginger and Courgettes

Ingredients for 6 servings

115 g/4 ounces/½ cup chickpea (gram) flour, sieved

250 ml/9 fluid oz/1 cup water

1 medium courgette (zucchini) fairly thinly sliced

4 spring onions (scallions) including the green part, very thinly sliced

4 cloves garlic, finely chopped

1 tbsp finely grated fresh ginger

Extra virgin olive oil

Instructions

Stir the water into the gram flour a little at a time, until it is all incorporated and the mixture is smooth. Stir in the grated ginger. Don't be alarmed at how watery the mixture is—it will puff up nicely.

Fry the courgette slices in 2-3 tbsp olive oil over a medium heat on each side for 2 minutes until golden, using a frying pan with a 9½ inch diameter. Remove from the pan, then add the onion and garlic. Stir and fry gently for 2 minutes until soft but not brown. Replace the courgettes in the pan and arrange the contents of the pan evenly over the bottom. Give the gram flour, ginger and water mixture a final stirring, then pour it carefully into the hot frying pan. Scramble the ingredients at the bottom of the pan very gently and briefly with a spoon, then cover the pan tightly and leave over a low to moderate heat for

What It's Good For

Gram (chick pea) flour is very rich in protein, and in this dish makes a delicious replacement for eggs, which are normally used to make frittata (a type of thick, round omelette). It is also a good source of many other nutrients, including calcium, magnesium, iron, copper and some of the B vitamins. Ginger is a wonderful aid to digestion. In Chinese medicine it is considered to warm the circulation and to combat catarrh and bronchitis.

Tip

Cut any hard bits off a big piece of ginger then grate it all and freeze teaspoonfuls in the individual wells of ice cube trays. (The skin is so delicate you don't need to peel it.)

15 minutes, until the sides and bottom of the frittata are golden brown and the top is set.

Slide the frittata on to a large plate, put another plate over the top, invert, then slide the frittata back into the frying pan to cook the other side for 5 minutes.

Serve the frittata warm or cold, cut into wedges and garnished with watercress.

Potato Wedges Roasted with Olive Oil and Garlic

Ingredients for each serving

1 medium potato, scrubbed

1 clove garlic, chopped

2 tbsp extra virgin olive oil

1 tsp low-sodium salt

Cayenne pepper

Instructions

Preheat the oven to 200°C/400°F/gas mark 6.

Pound the chopped garlic with the salt until smooth, using a mortar and pestle, then stir in the olive oil and cayenne pepper. Put this mixture in a shallow, oven-proof dish large enough to hold the potato wedges.

Bring one inch of water to the boil in a saucepan with a steamer basket.

Leave the skins on the potatoes. Cut each potato into half lengthwise and each half into four long wedges. Put the potato wedges in the steamer and steam over a medium heat for five minutes. Remove the wedges and brush each one with the oil and garlic mixture, ensuring it is thoroughly coated.

Arrange the wedges peeled side down in the dish and roast for 30 minutes. Baste after 15 minutes by dipping a basting brush into the oil, and brushing the wedges with it before returning the dish to the oven.

Serve as a snack dipped in hummus (page 79) or eggplant caviar (page 72).

What It's Good For

Potatoes are rich in potassium and many other nutrients. They also contain a small amount of vitamin C. Cooking them in this way, with a little olive oil, is an excellent way to make them crunchy and get all their goodness without the excessive fat of deep-frying

Hummus

Ingredients for 4 servings

1½ cups freshly cooked
  chickpeas (still warm)

½ cup cooking liquid from the
  chickpeas

2 heaped tbsp sesame seeds

4 tbsp extra virgin olive oil

1 tbsp lemon juice

1 clove garlic, crushed

½ tsp low-sodium salt

Cayenne pepper to taste

Instructions

Blend all the ingredients together in a food processor, adding more cooking liquid if necessary, until the mixture achieves the consistency of a thick dip.

Use as a dip for crudités (page 103) or roast potato wedges (page 78) or combine with shredded lettuce, peanuts, green pepper strips and grated radish and tuck into a flatbread (page 216).

What It's Good For

Chickpeas are very rich in protein, and are also a good source of many other nutrients, including calcium, magnesium, iron, copper and some of the B vitamins. Sesame seeds are one of the best available sources of calcium and magnesium, and also provide protein and zinc. They are one of the few good plant sources of the amino acid methionine. Research shows that they can help to lower cholesterol levels in the body.

Plum and Spring Onion Sushi

Ingredients to make 32 pieces

2 sheets of nori* approx 19x20 cm/7½x8 inches, cut in half

Approx 16 tbsp short-grain brown rice boiled for an extra 5 minutes until it is a little sticky

4 ready-to-eat (firm) prunes which have been marinaded for 2 hours in 3 tbsp tamari sauce and 1 tbsp rice wine vinegar (or cider vinegar)

2 spring onions (scallions), cut into 1-inch segments then finely shredded lengthwise

1 tsp wasabi sauce or ½ tsp wasabi powder

Instructions

Remove the prunes from the marinade, cut them into thin strips, and mix the wasabi with the rest of the marinade.

Place a half-sheet of nori on a clean tea towel, with the long edge towards you, and spread 2 tbsp of the cooked rice in a line along the centre from left to right. Lay a quarter of the prune strips on top of the rice followed by a quarter of the spring onion shreds. Carefully spread 2 more tbsp of rice over the top. Sprinkle with some of the marinade.

Now press the rice mixture down as firmly as you can with a fork. Roll the nori around the filling just like pastry round sausage meat. Moisten one edge so that the edge of the nori will stick to the other edge. It may take a little practice to get the quantity of rice filling just right so that it all fits in the nori sheet.

Put the sushi roll to one side, resting on

What It's Good For

Like most seafood, seaweed is rich in iodine, a trace mineral needed by your thyroid gland. Iodine is no longer routinely added to salt in many countries. Most people get it from dairy produce; iodine is used to sterilize the teats of cows before milking! Iodine deficiency is linked with higher rates of breast diseases. Japanese women, who eat a diet rich in iodine (including sushi) have always had a low rate of breast cancer. Iodine deficiency may also cause damage to nerves required for hearing.

*Nori are thin but strong and flexible sheets of pressed seaweed. They can be bought from health food stores.

Umeboshi plum sauce is available from shops which sell Japanese condiments.

its seam, while you make the others. When you are ready to serve the sushi, cut the roll into 8 or more bite-sized segments, using a very sharp knife.

Alternative filling

Sticky rice plus cucumber and cooked carrot strips flavoured with umeboshi plum sauce.

Miniature Baked Omelettes with Four Fillings

Ingredients for 4 servings

1 x 250 g pack/8½ ounces/
generous 1 cup standard (not
silken) firm tofu

4 tbsp soy or nut milk

Tamari sauce

Low-sodium salt & freshly ground
black pepper

**For the parsley and
mushroom filling**

3 medium white mushrooms,
finely chopped and fried in a
little olive oil for 1-2 minutes

1 tsp fresh, finely chopped parsley

For the shallot filling

1 medium shallot, finely diced and
gently fried in olive oil until
soft but not brown.

**For the carrot, ginger and
seaweed filling**

1 tbsp carrot grated into fine
shreds

2 inch square piece of nori
seaweed

1 tsp fresh grated ginger

**For the sun-dried tomato and
basil filling**

3 large basil leaves, finely
shredded

1 medium piece sun-dried tomato,
finely shredded

Instructions

Preheat the oven to 200°C/400°F/gas mark 6, and oil 12 wells of a mini-muffin tin.

Toast the nori sheet quickly under a hot grill (broiler) until it lightens in colour and turns crispy. Break into small pieces.

Using the S-blade of your food processor, whizz the tofu with the soy or nut milk, low-sodium salt and a few dashes of tamari sauce until creamy-smooth. This may take a few minutes. Scrape down the sides with a spatula from time to time.

Divide the mixture equally between four small bowls. To each bowl, add the ingredients for each of the fillings, plus a little black pepper, and stir together well.

Using two teaspoons, drop the mixture in the wells of the oiled mini-muffin tin and smooth down the surface. Bake in the oven for 20-25 minutes or until firm and springy and beginning to turn golden on top. Serve hot or cold on a bed of shredded lettuce, with some fruit chutney.

Try inventing some fillings of your own.

What It's Good For

See page 40 for some of the health benefits of soy. The taste and texture of this dish is remarkably like a real omelette.

Creamy Butternut Soup

Ingredients for 4 servings

1 medium butternut squash

1 litre/1¾ pints/4 cups soy or
  nut milk

1 large onion, finely chopped

2 tbsp extra virgin olive oil

Freshly ground black pepper

Instructions

Preheat the oven to 180°C/350°F/gas mark 4.

Cut the squash in half lengthwise, and remove the seeds with a spoon. Lay the squash pieces cut side down on a greased baking tray and bake in the preheated oven for 30 minutes or until soft.

Meanwhile sweat the onion in the olive oil in a large, heavy-bottomed saucepan over a low heat.

When the squash is ready, peel off the outside skin, chop the flesh and add it to the pan of onions, stir and heat through then add the soy or nut milk. Bring almost to the boil, stirring from time to time.

Using a hand blender, whizz the ingredients together until smooth and creamy.

If you find the soup a little too thick, you can add some water to correct the consistency.

What It's Good For

Like carrots and orange sweet potatoes, butternut squash are rich in cancer-preventing carotenes.

The best thing about this soup is that it tastes like something made with lavish amounts of cream, yet it is quite low in calories

Speciality Pâtés

The Basic Mixture

Makes 4 Servings

115 g/4 ounces/½ cup dried butterbeans (lima beans)

40 grams coconut oil

If you use refined coconut oil there will be no taste of coconut. Only virgin coconut oil has a coconut flavour.

Instructions

Cover the beans with four times their volume in boiling water and leave to soak overnight. Drain and place in a pressure cooker over a high heat with plenty of water to cover the beans generously. Put the lid on and bring the pressure cooker up to full steam. Cook for 6 to 10 minutes, depending on the age of the beans, then turn off the heat and immediately plunge the base of the pressure cooker into a sink of cold water. Once the pressure has reduced and you can open the lid, check that the beans are soft and tender by eating one. Do not allow the beans to cool down before you carry out the next stage, otherwise the coconut oil will not melt when you try to whizz it with the beans.

Transfer the hot beans and the coconut oil to a food processor. Using the S blade, process them until smooth and creamy. This may take several minutes. Scrape the sides down with a rubber spatula from time to time.

This basic mixture is flavoured by adding other ingredients

- Either to the food processor while blending
- Or to the finished product, by mashing them in roughly.

Poached Salmon and Dill Pâté

Ingredients for 4 servings

1 quantity of basic pâté mix

60 g/2 ounces fresh filleted salmon

1 tsp fresh dill, chopped

2 tsp fresh lemon juice

Low-sodium salt

Freshly ground black pepper

Instructions

Stir the lemon juice and seasoning into the basic pâté mix and incorporate thoroughly. Poach the fish in a few tablespoons of water for 5 minutes in a small covered pan. The salmon is cooked when it flakes easily. Drain the salmon and flake it, then mash it roughly into the basic pâté mix together with the chopped dill.

Mushroom and Garlic Pâté

Ingredients for 4 servings

One quantity of basic pâté mix

115 g/4 ounces/1 cup mushrooms, chopped

½ clove garlic, chopped

Extra virgin olive oil

Tamari sauce

Freshly ground black pepper

Instructions

Use mushrooms which have developed some black gills, as this helps to give this pâté a good colour.

Fry the chopped mushrooms in olive oil until golden. Whizz the mushrooms and garlic with the pâté mix and a few dashes of tamari sauce in a food processor until smooth. Stir in the black pepper.

What It's Good For

Beans are rich in protein. Try to use a cold-pressed, unrefined sunflower oil rather than supermarket oils, which are usually bleached and chemically treated to improve their shelf life. Unrefined oils should be as fresh as possible since they do not keep as well as refined oils.

Italian Herb Pâté

Ingredients for 4 servings

1 quanity of basic pâté mix

2 tbsp chopped fresh basil or pesto sauce (page 166)

Low-sodium salt

Freshly ground black pepper

Instructions

Whizz these ingredients together in a food processor or mash by hand.

Garlic, Chilli and Tomato Pâté

Ingredients for 4 servings

One quantity of basic pâté mix

1 tbsp tomato purée (paste)

½ clove garlic

½ tsp cayenne pepper

Low-sodium salt

Instructions

Stir the ingredients together until thoroughly incorporated.

How to serve the speciality pâtés

Spread on gluten-free toast, pumpernickel, rice cakes, oat cakes, corn crackers or pure rye crispbread such as Ryvita.

Mix with salad ingredients such as alfalfa sprouts, spread on warm pancakes (see page 140) and roll up like a Swiss roll. Keep warm until ready to serve.

Make canapés by squeezing the pâté from an icing bag on to cucumber slices. Top with half an olive.

Spread freshly-cooked polenta in a well-oiled large dish or tray into a thin layer. When cold, cut out small rounds of polenta, fry in hot olive oil until golden, then top with pâté and a sprinkling of fresh herbs or finely diced sweet peppers. Serve immediately.

Fill ramekin dishes with the pâtés and serve as a starter for spreading on crudités (pieces of raw carrot, celery, radish etc.).

The pâtés are liable to discolour slightly if left exposed for too long. You cannot entirely prevent this but it helps to whizz a tablespoon of fresh lemon juice into the basic mix.

Delicious Dips

Serve the dips with:

- Mini-poppadoms
- Pieces of flatbread

- Stick of raw vegetables
- Corn chips
- Potato wedges

- As a dressing for salads
- As a topping for baked potatoes.

Avocado Dip

Ingredients for 4 servings

1 quanity of basic pâté mix

1 avocado, roughly chopped

2 tsp fresh lemon juice

Freshly ground black pepper

Instructions

For the basic pâté mix use 75 ml sunflower oil instead of coconut oil.

Whizz all the ingredients together in a food processor until smooth.

Carrot and Corlander Dip

Ingredients for 4 servings

One quantity of basic pâté mix

1 large carrot, cut up and roasted

2 tbsp coriander (cilantro) leaves, finely chopped

½ tsp cayenne pepper

Low-sodium salt

Instructions

For the basic pâté mix use 75 ml sunflower oil instead of coconut oil.

Stir the ingredients together until thoroughly incorporated.

Try Some Ideas of Your Own

Lots of vegetables can be used to make delicious dips. Broccoli is especially delicious. Just peel the stem of a small head of broccoli, cut into small pieces and separate the head into small florets. Then steam until tender and whizz into the basic pâté mix. Try it with olives, onions or shallots, asparagus, artichokes, or roasted sweet peppers. Add herbs and spices to taste. Dips are made using added ingredients with a fairly high water content and so are softer than pâtés.

Spiced Bean Röstis

Ingredients for 2 servings

225 g/½ lb/1 cup cooked
black-eyed beans

½ small onion, finely chopped
or grated

3 medium-sized starchy (i.e.
non-waxy) potatoes

½ tbsp thick soy yoghurt

½ tsp curry powder

Olive oil

Low-sodium salt

Ground black pepper

Instructions

Peel and grate the potatoes, putting the gratings into a bowl of cold water. Mash the beans thoroughly and mix or blend in a food processor with the remaining ingredients except the olive oil and potato. Form the bean mixture into 4 patties. Using your hands, squeeze out the excess water from the grated potato and lay it on a clean tea towel. Fold the tea towel over and press the potatoes again to dry them as much as possible. Put the grated potatoes on a large plate. Place the bean patties on top of the potatoes, and press down gently. Cover the tops of the potatoes with as much grated potato as you can and press gently again. The potato will create quite a ragged covering, but this will adhere to the mixture when you start to cook the patties. Put a heavy-bottomed frying pan over a moderate heat and add a few tbsp olive oil. Slide a spatula under each

What It's Good For

These little Röstis are delicious and packed with protein from the beans. (Leftover basic pâté mix works just as well). Beans are rich in an amino acid known as lysine, which is lacking in most plant foods. In the human body, lysine is also converted into carnitine, an amino acid which helps to transport fat and convert it into energy. Vegetarians and vegans should eat beans and lentils regularly to avoid developing a lysine deficiency.

rösti to transfer it to the pan, and cook for about 5 minutes each side or until the potato is brown and crisp. Serve immediately with a mixed salad and a spoonful of Cacik (page 217) or Garlic Crème (page 206).

Recipe by Carolyn Gibbs

Danish Open Sandwiches (Smørrebrød)

Open sandwiches are made with only one slice of bread (in this case pumpernickel), piled high with delicacies, and eaten with a knife and fork. Prepare ingredients according to how many people you are catering for.

Salmon and Potato Salad Topping

Ingredients

Wheat- and yeast-free
   pumpernickel bread*

Fresh salmon, filleted

Potato salad (see page 176)
   made with finely diced
   potatoes

Mayonnaise (see page 210)

Fresh dill herb

*This is a black rye bread with a strong, sweet flavour, ideal for open sandwiches. It is easily available from supermarkets and delicatessens.

Instructions

Poach the salmon fillet by putting it in a small saucepan with a few tablespoons of water and cooking with the lid on for 5-10 minutes over a gentle heat until the fish is opaque throughout and flakes easily.

Remove the fish with a slotted spoon and allow to cool. Separate into large flakes. Gently fold the salmon flakes into the potato salad.

Spread a spoonful of mayonnaise on to a slice of pumpernickel, then add a large dollop of the potato salad and salmon mixture. Finish with a sprinkling of chopped dill.

Recipe by Carolyn Gibbs

What It's Good For

Dianne Onstad's *Whole Foods Companion* tells us that the basic bread of medieval Britain consisted of coarsely ground rye and pea flours, sometimes with a little barley flour mixed in. Rye is most popular in Russia, as it tolerates the severe climate better than other grains. Wholegrain rye is rich in B vitamins, magnesium, iron and zinc, and as its fibre absorbs water well, it is excellent for bowel health. Black rye breads are made by cooking the bread at a relatively low temperature for a long time.

Hummus and Rainbow Salad Topping

Ingredients

Wheat- and yeast-free
  pumpernickel bread

Hummus (see page 79)

Mayonnaise

Gherkins, drained, well-rinsed
  and finely sliced

Grated carrot

Grated raw beetroot

Cherry tomatoes, sliced

Red sweet (bell) pepper, very
  finely diced

Yellow sweet (bell) pepper,
  very finely diced

Lettuce leaves, finely
  shredded

Spring onion (scallion), finely
  sliced

Fresh flat-leaf parsley,
  chopped

Instructions

Spread a generous layer of hummus on a slice of pumpernickel. Cover with sliced gherkins. Mix together the grated carrot and beetroot, cherry tomato slices and a sprinkling of the diced peppers, using a little mayonnaise to bind the mixture, and spoon it on top of the gherkins. Finish with a sprinkling of spring onion (scallion).

Recipe by Carolyn Gibbs

What It's Good For

Why not make up some open sandwich toppings of your own? The Speciality Pâtés and Crab Terrine also make a delicious base and can be topped with chopped gherkins, capers, spring onion, (scallion), pickled garlic, alfalfa sprouts and Sour Cream (page 205) or Garlic Crème (page 206).

Guacamole

Ingredients for 2-4 servings

1 small, ripe avocado

1 medium tomato, skinned, deseeded and finely chopped

½ green chilli pepper (seeds removed), very thinly sliced

2 tbsp mayonnaise (see page 210)

1 tbsp fresh lemon juice

½ clove garlic, crushed

Low-sodium salt

Instructions

Scoop the flesh out of the avocado and, using a fork, immediately mash the lemon juice into it.

Keep mashing until no large lumps remain, then stir in the crushed garlic and low-sodium salt until thoroughly incorporated, followed by the mayonnaise and then the chopped tomato and chilli pepper.

Serve as a starter or as part of a buffet meal, with tortilla chips or wheat-free crispbread or crackers to dip in the guacamole, or put spoonfuls on to little squares of warm flatbread (see page 216).

What It's Good For

Described as one of nature's most perfect foods, creamy, buttery avocados are so nutritious that they are practically a whole meal in themselves. They are easy to digest, and rich in protein, omega 6 polyunsaturated oils, vitamin B6 and other B vitamins, vitamin E, iron and copper, with three times as much potassium as bananas. The rough-skinned Hass avocado has a particularly good flavour. The raw garlic in this recipe will help people with intestinal bacterial imbalances.

French Onion Soup

Ingredients for 2 servings

2 medium onions, peeled, cut in half vertically then thinly sliced

2 tbsp extra virgin olive oil

560 ml/1 pint/2 cups boiling water

1 heaped tbsp wheat-free miso*

Herbs to taste: thyme, bay leaves and parsley are all suitable

Freshly ground black pepper

*Miso is a traditional Japanese food in health food stores. oriental shops and larger supermarkets. It is made from soybeans and has a meaty flavour and a brown colour, very suitable as a tasty substitute for beef stock. In Japan is is often mixed with boiling water and drunk as a thin soup.

Instructions

Heat the oil in a large saucepan over a medium heat, then add the onions and gently stir-fry for about 20 minutes until beginning to caramelize.

Add the water followed by the miso and the herbs. Stir well to dissolve the miso.

Bring the liquid back to the boil, cover, and simmer over a low heat for 30 minutes. Season with freshly-ground black pepper before serving.

What It's Good For

The therapeutic value of the humble onion is often forgotten in favour of its famous cousin garlic. Onions are a rich source of the anti-allergy flavonoid quercetin, which is very similar to the drug disodium chromoglycate given to switch off allergic symptoms. Like the drug, quercetin can inhibit the release of histamine, the cause of allergic symptoms, inflammation and asthma attacks. Quercetin has also been investigated for its virus-fighting properties.

Falafel (chickpea patties)

Ingredients to make 8-9 small patties

115 g/4 ounces dried chickpeas which have been covered with four times their volume in boiling water and soaked overnight

1 medium onion, cut into 8 pieces

2 tbsp fresh coriander (cilantro) leaves, finely chopped

2 cloves garlic, roughly chopped

1 tsp coriander seeds

1 tsp cumin seeds

¼ tsp baking powder

Low-sodium salt

Cayenne pepper

Olive oil for frying

Instructions

Drain the soaked chickpeas, and, using the S blade, whizz them in a food processor with the onion and garlic until they become a smooth paste which clumps together. Roughly crush the coriander and cumin seeds with a mortar and pestle then dry-roast them in a medium-hot frying pan for about half a minute to release the aromas. Stir the spices, seasonings and baking powder into the chickpea mixture and mix thoroughly.

Preheat a frying pan over a medium heat and pour in olive oil to coat the bottom of the pan. Take tablespoons of the chickpea mixture, and, using your hands, form them into little patties measuring about 2 inches in diameter. When the oil is hot, gently lower the patties into it and cook for about 5 minutes on each side. Handle them gently when turning them over—I use a pair of flat tongs such as

What It's Good For

Chickpeas are very rich in protein, and are a good source of many other nutrients, including calcium, magnesium, iron, copper and some of the B vitamins. Falafels are a Middle Eastern dish and are often served stuffed into pitta bread and topped with salad and yoghurt. Always buy pulses/ legumes (members of the bean and lentil family) with the longest 'sell- by' date you can find. Lengthy storage makes them tough and they will take longer to cook.

those used for turning fried fish. Drain the falafels on absorbent kitchen paper and serve hot or cold as a starter, snack, packed lunch or light supper dish with Cacik (page 217) and a green salad, or tucked into flatbread (page 216) and topped with shredded lettuce and Garlic Crème (page 206).

Spinach and Lentil Soup

Ingredients for 6 servings

1.2 litres/2 pints/4 cups water

115g/4 ounces/½ cup brown
lentils or Puy lentils*

250 g/9 ounces fresh spinach

1 large onion, chopped

2 tbsp miso

1 tbsp tomato purée (paste)

1 tbsp fresh lemon juice

Freshly ground black pepper

Salt is not needed as miso is naturally salty.

*These are small green speckled lentils. They are best for this soup as they retain a slightly chewy texture which contrasts well with the smoothness of the spinach.

Instructions

Put the water, lentils and chopped onion in a large saucepan and bring to the boil, then cover the pan and simmer gently for 30 minutes.

Meanwhile, wash and drain the spinach. Twist off any tough, fibrous stalks then take bundles of leaves, and shred them coarsely with a knife. Turn the shredded spinach bundles round 90 degrees and shred crosswise so that the spinach ends up roughly chopped.

When the lentils are ready, stir in the miso and tomato paste, then stir in the spinach. Put the lid on and leave over a low heat for 5 minutes or until the spinach has wilted and softened.

Using a hand blender, briefly whizz the soup while still in the pan, so that most of the lentils are still a little chewy, while the rest of the soup is thick and smooth. Stir in the freshly ground black pepper.

What It's Good For

Spinach and lentils are good sources of an important B vitamin known as folic acid. This is likely to be in short supply in a diet consisting mostly of convenience foods because it is easily destroyed by food processing and lengthy storage. Spinach is also an excellent source of iron, but remember that iron from plant foods is not well absorbed unless the meal also contains vitamin C. The lemon juice in this recipe will help you absorb the iron, and you could also finish the meal with some fresh fruit.

Red Lentil and Chestnut Soup with Cumin and Parsley

Ingredients for 2 servings

150 ml/¼ pint/½ cup red lentils measured in a measuring jug

600 ml/1 pint/2 cups water

8 vacuum-packed chestnuts*

1 medium onion, chopped

2 tbsp olive oil

1 tbsp miso

1 tbsp chopped fresh parsley

½ tsp cumin seeds, roughly crushed with a mortar and pestle

Low-sodium salt

Freshly ground black pepper

*You could also use fresh chestnuts. Boil until tender and peel while hot.

Instructions

Put the water and lentils in a saucepan and bring to the boil. Squash the chestnuts gently with the heel of your hand so that they will break up a little when cooking.

Meanwhile in a separate pan fry the onions in the olive oil over a medium heat until beginning to soften. Add the cumin and stir-fry until the aroma is released.

Add the contents of the pan to the lentils along with the chestnuts and simmer together for 45 minutes. Just before serving, add the seasoning and parsley.

What It's Good For

I like to use red onions for this recipe. The red colour is anthocyanin, a good antioxidant. Chestnuts are low in oil and are nutritionally quite similar to grains such as corn or rice. They are a good source of potassium, magnesium and iron. If lentils make you 'windy' (as they do with most people), follow your meal with Digestive Tea (page 222).

Potato Pancakes with a Spinach, Mushroom and Goat's Cheese Filling

Ingredients to make 1 pancake

2 medium-sized waxy
    potatoes

55 g/2 ounces/½ cup
    mushrooms, thinly sliced*

25 g/1 ounce hard goat's
    cheese, finely grated

50 g spinach, washed and
    shredded

Olive oil

Freshly ground black pepper

*You could use some of the
more unusual varieties of
mushrooms such as shiitake if
you would like a change.

Instructions

Preheat a 25 cm/9½ inch diameter frying pan over a medium heat until very hot, then add 2 tbsp oil.

Coarsely grate the potatoes as quickly as you can to prevent browning, then transfer them to the hot frying pan. Using the tip of a spatula, distribute them evenly in the pan and press down to flatten. Cover the frying pan and leave the pancake to cook for one minute then turn the heat down low-medium and leave it to cook for a further 9 minutes.

Remove the pan from the heat and carefully slide the pancake on to a large plate. Cover the pancake with a second plate, then invert the plates, thus turning the pancake over. Replace the pan over a medium heat. When hot, add another tbsp oil, then carefully slide the pancake back into the pan to cook the other side and replace the lid. Turn the heat down again after one minute and then cook for a further 5 minutes. Remove from the pan and keep warm.

What It's Good For

Waxy potatoes allow you to make a deliciously succulent pancake without the need for egg. Potatoes are rich in potassium, and also lysine, a protein constituent (amino acid) which is low in most plant foods except beans and lentils, and is especially needed by herpes sufferers. Goat's cheese is also a good source of protein (including lysine). Spinach is a wonderful source of iron and other minerals, and mushrooms provide B vitamins and chromium.

While the pancake is cooking, stir-fry the mushrooms in 2 tbsp hot olive oil until golden. Stir in the shredded spinach and toss until wilted. Remove from the heat and spoon on to one half of the potato pancake. Cover with grated cheese, season with freshly ground black pepper then fold the other half of the pancake over the filling and serve.

Potato Pancakes with a Mexican Filling

Ingredients to make 4-8 portions

2 potato pancakes made as described on page 98

2 avocados

1 quantity of refried beans made as described on page 122

1 tsp lemon juice

Low-sodium salt

Freshly ground black pepper

Instructions

Preheat the oven to 200°C/400°F/Gas mark 6.

Peel and mash the avocados with the lemon juice. Season with low-sodium salt and pepper. Spread one of the potato pancakes with this mixture.

Spread the other potato pancake with the warm refried beans.

Sandwich the pancakes together, with the fillings in the middle.

Place on a baking tray and heat in the oven for 10-15 minutes.

Serve cut into wedges on a bed of lettuce.

What It's Good For

Delicious buttery avocadoes are rich in protein, omega 6 essential polyunsaturated oils, vitamin B6 and other B vitamins, vitamin E, iron and copper, and provide three tiems as much potassium as bananas. They are also easy to digest. Beans are also a good source of protein— one of the few good plant sources of the amino acid lysine, needed for your body to produce carnitine which helps you metabolize the fats and oils in your diet and turn them into energy.

Spring Greens Braised with Potatoes and Red Onions, with a Sour Cream Topping

Ingredients to make 2 servings

2 large potatoes, diced small

4 large leaves from a head of spring (collard) greens, cut crosswise into thin ribbons

1 medium red onion, cut in half lengthwise then thinly sliced

1 inch piece of root ginger, shredded (optional)

Spice mixture to taste (e.g. any combination of ground black pepper, cardamom, fennel, cloves, coriander seeds (optional)

A quantity of sour cream made as described on page 205

Fresh chives, finely chopped

2 tbsp olive oil

Low-sodium salt

Instructions

Using a large saucepan or sauté pan with a heavy base, fry the onion in the olive oil over a medium heat. When beginning to soften, add the spices (if using), heat through, then the potatoes and ginger (if using). Stir-fry together for one minute. Stir in the spring greens. Add 3 tbsp water, and season with low-sodium salt.

Cover the pan tightly, and cook over the lowest heat for 30 minutes, checking from time to time that there is enough moisture to prevent the contents from burning. If necessary add a little more water.

When all the ingredients are tender, all remaining moisture should be boiled off by removing the lid and turning up the heat. Turn out on to a plate and top with Sour Cream sprinkled with fresh chives and ground black pepper.

What It's Good For

Spring or collard greens are a rich source of folic acid, magnesium, iron and lutein—the carotene which plays an important part in your eyesight.

Without enough folic acid you can become depressed because your body cannot turn the amino acids tyrosine and tryptophan into adrenal hormones and serotonin, respectively. Many psychiatric patients are found to have a folic acid deficiency.

Crudités

Ingredients for 2 servings

1 large carrot

1 large green (bell) pepper

1 large sweet red (bell) pepper

2 stalks of celery

Half a mooli/daikon* radish

Half a cucumber

*Mooli/daikon radishes are long, white radishes about twice the size of carrots. They are often used in Oriental cookery, and can be found in larger supermarkets. If you cannot obtain one, use ordinary radishes.

Instructions

Cut the radish and carrot into 6 cm/3 inch segments then slice these lengthwise first one way and then the other to make sticks.

Cut around the stalk of the peppers and remove it, then cut the peppers into eight pieces lengthwise. Discard the seeds but retain as much of the white pith as possible.

Using a sharp knife or vegetable peeler, peel the outside of the celery stalks so that the tough fibres are stripped away, then cut the stalks in half.

Cut the cucumber into 6 cm/3 inch segments then cut each segment into four pieces lengthwise.

Arrange the crudités on a plate, with a selection of dips for people to help themselves.

Suitable dips from this book are those on page 87 and also:

- Sour cream (page 205)
- Hummus (page 79)
- Garlic crème (page 206).

What It's Good For

Delicious crunchy raw vegetables are an ideal party snack. Among other this, this dish provides: Carrots—beta carotene; Peppers—vitamin C and flavonoids; Celery—organic sodium (unlike sodium from salt, this is not harmful) and coumarins, which help to release fluid retention; Cucumber—silicon (good for bone and skin strength); Mooli/daikon radish—sulphur compounds, which are highly beneficial for the liver.

Crab Terrine

Ingredients for 4-6 servings

1 medium-sized crab, dressed*

115 g/4 ounces silken tofu (see page 246)

2 tbsp sunflower oil

15 g/½ ounce gelatine powder

Soy or sheep's milk yoghurt as required

1 tbsp fresh lemon juice

3 tbsp water

Low-sodium salt

Freshly ground black pepper

*You can either buy the crab ready-dressed, or, for a better flavour, dress it yourself just before making this recipe (see next page).

Instructions

Put the 3 tbsp water in a small dish, and sprinkle the gelatine powder over it to soften.

Whizz the silken tofu, brown crab meat, sunflower oil, low-sodium salt and lemon juice until smooth, in a food processor using the S blade. If you are using a firm variety of silken tofu such as Sanchi Organic Tofu, you will also need to add 2 tbsp of water to soften the consistency.

Heat 2 tbsp water in a small saucepan over a moderate heat until it is boiling vigorously, then remove it from the heat, empty out the water and immediately put the softened gelatine into the hot pan. If the pan retains heat well, the gelatine should then dissolve and quickly become runny when stirred. (If it does not, you will need to boil some water in a larger pan and then put the smaller pan inside it so that you can heat the gelatine to the runny stage without scorching it).

What It's Good For

As they grow larger, crabs have to grow a new (soft) shell inside the old one. This soft shell can be scraped out and is not only delicious but extremely nutritious and full of the bone-nourishing minerals calcium, magnesium and zinc. Crabs are also an exceptionally good source of iodine and selenium, trace elements which are very depleted in British crops. Both are important for your thyroid gland, which governs your metabolism. Low Iodine levels can increase the risk of breast disease in women.

Dressing a Crab

Ask the fishmonger to prise it open for you if you don't know how to do this, and to remove the inedible 'dead men's fingers' (contrary to popular belief, they are not poisonous). Ask for a male crab if you want one with more white meat.

Dressing a crab just means prising the meat out from every little nook and cranny. It can take up to an hour. Keeping the white meat separate from the brown meat (which is also known as the 'cream' of the crab) use strong kitchen scissors to cut through the internal body shell and up the small leg segments before prising them open, and a skewer to ease out the meat. Crack the large claws with a hammer.

Pour some of the whizzed crab mixture into the pan of gelatine and stir thoroughly, then pour this mixture back into the food processor with the rest. Process again briefly until the gelatine has been thoroughly incorporated, scraping down the sides with a rubber spatula half-way through.

Then, using the same spatula, scrape the crab mixture into a measuring jug with a capacity of at least one pint (570 ml) and fold in the shredded white crab meat. If the contents of the jug do not reach the 1 pint mark, top them up with soy or sheep's yoghurt.

Season with freshly ground black pepper, mix well, then pour into a small loaf tin or long plastic mould which has been lined with clingfilm. Chill for several hours before serving.

Serving suggestions

- Cut into slabs and serve as a starter on shredded lettuce with wheat-free crispbread or crackers,

- Dollop on to crispy potato cakes (page 164) as a delicious topping.

More About Selenium

Scientists now know that people who eat a selenium-rich diet have a much lower risk of getting a heart attack or cancer. Selenium should be absorbed from the soil into our cereal crops, but the soil in most areas of the UK, New Zealand, Finland and parts of China are very poor in selenium. So we have to make up for it by consuming more Brazil nuts, seafood and selenium supplements. Selenium also helps to activate thyroid hormone and to make an antioxidant enzyme, glutathione peroxidase.

Potato Ravioli

Ingredients for about 24 small ravioli (2 servings)

One quantity of Potato Gnocci dough (see page 170)

2 tbsp pesto sauce (page 166)

25 g/1 ounce finely grated goat's cheese* for filling plus 55 g/2 ounces for topping

*Choose a hard variety that grates easily

Instructions

Divide the potato dough in half and form each half into a ball. Using a rolling pin, roll out the dough ball into a sheet about ½ cm/¼ inch thick.

Using a glass tumbler or pastry cutter with a diameter of about 5 cm/2½ inches, cut out as many rounds from this sheet as you can.

Bring a large saucepan of water to the boil.

Dot the centre of each round with a small blob of pesto sauce and a pinch of grated cheese, then fold the rounds over and, using the very tips of your fingers, carefully pinch the edges together to form a tiny 'pasty'.

You should not have trouble getting the edges to stay together if your pinches are tiny enough, but if you do you could dampen the edges of the rounds with a little water before pressing together.

What It's Good For

Based on my experience, I would say that about half of all people with a food intolerance have problems with cow's milk products. As with other food intolerances, these problems can be anything from headaches to eczema, joint pains or digestive problems. Substituting goat or sheep's milk, cheese and yoghurt is not the answer for everyone but go ahead and enjoy an occasional recipe like this if it does not cause you any symptoms.

As you prepare the ravioli, put them on a plate then gently slide them off the plate into the gently boiling water. Cook for 60-80 seconds then remove them from the water with a slotted spoon. Serve immediately, sprinkled with the rest of the grated cheese.

Lamb's Liver Terrine with Onions and Thyme

Ingredients for 4-6 servings

300 g/10 ounces organic lamb's liver, roughly cut into chunks

150 g/5 ounces onions, finely chopped

2 walnut-sized knobs of coconut oil

1 tsp dried thyme

Low-sodium salt

Freshly-ground black pepper

Instructions

Heat one knob of coconut oil in a frying pan over a medium heat, add the onions, and sweat them for 5 minutes until translucent.

Keeping the pan hot, transfer the onions into the bowl of a food processor fitted with the S blade, then add the second knob of coconut oil into the frying pan followed by the chunks of lamb's liver. Stir and fry for about 5 minutes, until cooked, then add the liver to the onions in the food processor. Season with low-sodium salt.

Scraping down the sides with a rubber spatula from time to time, whizz the liver and onions until the mixture is a fine paste.

While still warm, empty the mixture into a terrine dish with a capacity of about half a litre/¾ pint and smooth down the surface with a fork. Allow to cool and when cold cover the dish with a piece of

What It's Good For

Poisonous amounts of vitamin A are only found in intensively-reared animals—their feed contains artificially large amounts of vitamin A added as a growth-promoter. Their liver can end up containing 20 times the normal amount of vitamin A. Organic liver does not have this problem. Liver provides protein, vitamin A, B vitamins and many minerals including chromium and zinc. It is worth consuming it occasionally; not everyone is efficient at making vitamin A from beta carotene.

absorbent kitchen paper (to prevent condensation dripping on the contents) followed by a lid or a sheet of clingfilm, and place in the fridge for at least 3 hours. Serve slices of the terrine on wheat– and yeast-free crackers, crispbread or pumpernickel, or on a bed of lettuce with salad.

Bean, Potato and Goat Cheese Wraps

Ingredients for 2 wraps

2 flatbreads made using the
recipe on page 216
Half a can of cannellini
beans
4 spring onions (scallions)
thinly sliced (about 2
large handfuls)
1 small potato, diced small
A few knobs melting goats
cheese
1 clove garlic, chopped
Low-sodium salt
Freshly-ground black
pepper

A heavy-bottom pan such
as an enamelled cast iron
casserole dish is best for a
braised recipe like this one.
If you don't have one, a
small frying pan with lid
will do.

Instructions

Fry the sliced spring onions and chopped garlic gently in 3 tbsp olive oil until beginning to soften. Stir in the beans and the diced potato and seasoning. Add half a cup of water or stock and bring to the boil. Simmer gently on the lowest heat for 30 minutes until the ingredients are very tender. Check from time to time that there is still enough liquid to prevent the pan from drying out. If any liquid remains at the end, turn up the heat and boil it off quickly. When ready, stir in the goat's cheese. Spoon the mixture on to flatbreads and roll up.

Variation

You can also serve this recipe spooned into individual gluten-free tart cases to serve as a starter with a green salad.

Instead of potato you could use diced carrots or butternut squash.

Gluten-free flatbreads can also be purchased from supermarkets.

What It's Good For

Beans are a great source of vegetarian protein, and keep you feeling full due to their soluble fibre. These wraps make a nice alternative to sandwiches. Many places of work have a kitchen with a small oven and if so, you could take this wrap to work with you, wrapped in tin foil, and warm it in the oven before removing the foil to eat it.

Italian Bean Soup

Ingredients for 3 servings

2 cups of cooked borlotti beans*

1 litre/1¾ pints, 4 cups chicken or vegetable stock

1 shallot, chopped

1 cup shredded vegetables (e.g. carrot, cabbage, broccoli, peppers)

2 fresh tomatoes, finely chopped

3 tbsp olive oil

1 small fresh chilli pepper, chopped

1 tbsp chopped parsley

*Ensure the beans are very tender or they won't break down well. Beans home-cooked in a pressure cooker work well.

Instructions

In a large saucepan with a heavy bottom, fry the chopped shallot and chilli pepper gently in the olive oil until beginning to soften. Stir in 1 cup of beans and stir-fry gently until warmed through. Using a potato masher, mash the contents of the pan until the beans have been reduced to a paste.

Add the stock and shredded vegetables to the pan, stir, and bring to the boil. If the stock is unsalted you may need to season with low-sodium salt.

Simmer gently for 25 minutes, stirring occasionally. Now add the chopped tomatoes, parsley and remaining beans.

Return the pan to the heat until it is just about to boil, stir, then remove from the heat and serve.

What It's Good For

Borlotti beans are full of flavour and a great source of vegetarian protein. If you are trying to lose weight, this soup is filling and nutritious enough to be a one-pot meal. Two large bowls will likely fill you up for several hours, without loading you with calories. The high liquid content of soup means that it takes longer to digest, which is why you stay feeling full for much longer than with a normal meal.

Main Courses

Lots of people are confused about how much they should eat at different mealtimes.

The truth is, a heavy meal eaten late in the day is much more easily turned into body fat. This is because you would normally be sleeping at night and cannot use it up like your other meals.

The old maxim 'Breakfast like a King, lunch like a prince and dine like a pauper' is absolutely true.

Balkan Peppers Stuffed with a Bean Medley

Ingredients for 4 servings

2 capsicum (bell) peppers, washed

1 x 400g can/10 ounces/ 1 generous cup cooked mixed beans (haricot beans, pinto beans, chick peas etc.)

1 large onion, thinly sliced

1 stick celery, finely chopped

4 cloves garlic, chopped

200 ml water

2 tbsp olive oil

1 dessertspoon gluten-free or rice flour

1 heaped tsp paprika powder (not the hot variety)

1 tbsp fresh chopped parsley

Low-sodium salt

Freshly ground black pepper

Instructions

Preheat the oven to 180°C/350°F/gas mark 4. Cut the peppers in half, remove the stalks and centres, and stand the peppers open side up in a close-fitting deep dish. (If necessary cut a little off the bottom so that they can stand without falling over.)

Using a stir-fry pan or a large saucepan with a heavy base, fry the onions, celery and garlic over a medium heat for five minutes or until beginning to brown. Stir in the paprika, flour, parsley and seasonings. Add the water a little at a time, stirring to form a gravy. When all the water has been incorporated, fold in the beans.

Spoon the bean mixture into and around the half peppers. Cover the dish and place in the oven for one hour. By this time the peppers should be tender. Serve with creamed potatoes and a green salad.

Variation

Try adding chopped mushrooms instead of celery.

What It's Good For

A hearty dish for a winter's day, this brings you all the goodness of carotene from the peppers and protein from the beans. Paprika powder—used to make Hungarian goulash—is simply dried and powdered sweet capsicum (bell) peppers. These are a very popular crop in Eastern Europe. Housewives preserve and bottle peppers to last throughout the winter, and there are many wonderful and unusual preserving recipes combining different ingredients.

Organic Chicken Sauté with Vegetables and Garlic

Ingredients for 2 servings

2 medium portions organic chicken

1 x 400 g/14 ounce can chopped plum tomatoes

4 medium potatoes, peeled and cut in half

1 large onion, roughly diced

1 large carrot, cut into 1-inch segments

115 g/4 ounces/1 cup white mushrooms, thickly sliced

4 cloves garlic, peeled and roughly chopped

2 tbsp extra virgin olive oil

2 tbsp gluten-free flour

1 tbsp soy cream (optional)

Low-sodium salt

Black pepper

Instructions

This is a one-pot meal made in a pressure cooker. Season the chicken portions with low-sodium salt then coat thoroughly with the flour. Heat the olive oil in the pressure cooker with the lid off, then add the chicken pieces. Fry over a high heat until golden and crisp on both sides (this seals in the juices), then stir in the onion and garlic, and continue stirring until they begin to soften. Pour in the chopped tomatoes, stir, put the lid on and bring the pressure cooker up to full steam. Maintaining a steady pressure, cook for 20 minutes.

Put the pressure cooker in a sink of cold water to bring the pressure down and enable you to remove the lid. Stir the contents, then add the remaining vegetables to the pan, fitting them neatly around the chicken and ensuring they are all coated with the sauce. (If necessary add a little

What It's Good For

Even free-range chickens may be fed standard commercial feed which contains antibiotics, chicken dung and other unsavoury items. We do not know what residues remain in the bird's meat and fat, and how they affect our health. Eating organic chicken overcomes all these dilemmas. And the flavour is far better. Chicken is an excellent, low-fat source of protein—even with its skin left on. Protein is essential for all body processes, including the important detoxification work of your liver.

Special Equipment

A pressure cooker

water to the pan to enable this). Replace the lid and heat again to full steam. Once again maintaining a steady pressure, cook for a further 12 minutes.

Put the pressure cooker in cold water again and once it is safe to do so, remove the lid, check that the vegetables are tender, and remove the chicken and vegetable pieces to a heated serving dish with the aid of a slotted spoon. Keep warm. Replace the pressure cooker on the stove, without putting the lid on, and turn up the heat until you can fast-boil the sauce remaining in the pan. Keep stirring and reduce to about 2-3 ladlefuls of thick sauce. Remove from the heat and add 1 tbsp soy cream, plus some freshly ground black pepper. Stir through and pour the sauce over the chicken and vegetables. Serve immediately.

Variation

This recipe can also be adapted for cooking in the oven in a casserole dish.

This is a dish rich in many nutrients. Most notably Italian plum tomatoes, with their deep, rich red colour are the best source of lycopene, a type of carotene which due to its powerful antioxidant properties has been found to help prevent prostate cancer and also breast cancer. A similar antioxidant, beta carotene is found in carrots. The body can also convert beta carotene into vitamin A. Onions are a good source of the flavonoid quercetin, which helps to fight allergies. Mushrooms are one of the few natural good sources of chromium, a trace element needed for sugar and carbohydrate metabolism.

Baked Potatoes with Salmon and Sour Cream

Ingredients for 2 servings

2 baking potatoes, well scrubbed

115 g/4 ounces fresh (preferably wild) salmon, filleted

1 spring onion (scallion), finely sliced

Soy or nut milk

1 tsp fresh dill, chopped

Low-sodium salt

Freshly ground black pepper

Instructions

Preheat the oven to 200°C/400°F/Gas mark 6.

Prick the potatoes all over with a fork, and bake them for 45 minutes or until they feel soft when you squeeze them. Poach the salmon in a few tablespoons of water in a lidded pan over a low heat for five minutes, until the fish flakes easily.

Remove the potatoes from the oven and slice in half lengthways. Scoop out the potato flesh, leaving the skins intact. Mash the potato flesh with a little soy or nut milk and seasoning, then gently fold in the spring onion and salmon flakes, trying not to break them up too much, and pile the mixture into the potato skin halves. Return to the oven for 15 minutes to heat through, then serve with a generous topping of sour cream (see page 205) and a sprinkling of dill.

What It's Good For

Like herrings (see recipe on page 64, salmon is a so-called 'oily' fish, rich in omega 3 oils which help prevent red blood cells from clumping together and causing heart attacks. You may not know that these oily fish themselves are a far richer source of omega 3 oils than fish oil supplements. Wild salmon is also one of the few good sources of the powerful antioxidant astaxanthin. Astaxanthin has the dark red colour that is characteristic of wild salmon.

More ideas for baked potato toppings

- Chickpeas and guacamole (page 92)
- Pesto (page 166)
- Onion marmalade (page 157)
- Avocado and tomato in vinaigrette with chopped coriander (cilantro)

Baked Potatoes with Green Cabbage Courgettes and Red Onion

Ingredients for 2 servings

2 baking potatoes, well scrubbed

4 large leaves from a head of green cabbage, shredded cross-wise into ribbons

1 large courgette (zucchini), cut lengthwise into little sticks (use a julienne cutter if you have one)

1 red onion cut in half lengthwise and thinly sliced

4 tbsp sheep's milk yoghurt or thick soy yoghurt

2 tbsp olive oil

1 tbsp fresh chives, chopped

Low-sodium salt

Freshly ground black pepper

Instructions

Preheat the oven to 200°C/400°F/Gas mark 6.

Prick the potatoes all over with a fork, and bake them for 45 minutes or until they feel soft when you squeeze them.

Meanwhile make the topping. Stir the chives into the yoghurt and season with low-sodium salt and black pepper. Leave to one side.

In a large heavy-bottomed saucepan, gently stir-fry the onion slices in the olive oil for a minute or so until beginning to soften. Add the cabbage and courgette sticks, and stir-fry together for half a minute. Add 3 tbsp water, then cover the pan tightly and turn down the heat to the lowest setting. Cook for 15 minutes, checking occasionally that there is enough moisture in the pan to prevent burning.

What It's Good For

Dark green cabbage is one of the best sources of lutein, a type of carotene which helps to protect your eyesight. Lutein is hard to get from your diet unless you regularly eat deep green leafy vegetables. These are also a good source of magnesium, which is often lacking in the average diet.

Red onions contain anthocyanin—a powerful antioxidant with a blue colour that can also look red or purple in certain plants.

Remove from the heat and season with low-sodium salt and black pepper. Keep warm until the potatoes are ready.

Remove the potatoes from the oven and cut into quarters, but not all the way through. Open out the potatoes and pile on the vegetables. Top with the yoghurt and chive mixture.

Stuffed Sweet Peppers with Wild Rice and Porcini Mushrooms

Ingredients for 2 servings

2 medium to large sweet (bell) peppers (red, green or yellow)

125 g/4½ ounces/½ cup firm tofu

4 tbsp cooked brown rice, to include 1 tsp cooked wild or red rice

1 small to medium onion, finely chopped

1 small handful dried porcini mushrooms which have been soaked in boiling water for half an hour and then finely chopped

4 cloves garlic, finely chopped

2 tbsp soy or nut milk

2 tbsp extra virgin olive oil

1 tsp fresh basil, finely chopped

Low-sodium salt

Freshly ground black pepper

Instructions

Preheat the oven to 180°C/350°F/gas mark 4. Blanch the peppers for two minutes in a pan of boiling water then remove and drain. Sweat the chopped onion slowly in the olive oil over a low heat, with the lid on the pan. Cut the tops (with stalks) off the peppers and save them to make lids. Remove the seeds with a teaspoon.

In a blender or food processor (with S blade), whizz the tofu and soy or nut milk, scraping the sides down with a spatula from time to time, until smooth and creamy.

When the onions are soft, add the garlic, chopped mushrooms, cooked rice, basil and seasoning. Stir-fry together in the pan for half a minute, then fold in the creamed tofu. Remove from the heat, and keep folding with a spoon to ensure that all the ingredients are thoroughly incorporated.

What It's Good For

The main ingredients of this dish are tofu and sweet peppers. See page 40 for the benefits of tofu and other soy products. Sweet peppers are an excellent source of vitamin C and flavonoids. Many of the flavonoids are concentrated in the white pith, so try not to throw it away. Green sweet peppers are simply an unripe version of red ones, and contain less carotene.

Stuff the peppers with this mixture and press it in firmly. Replace the tops of the peppers. Stand the peppers up in an oiled oven-proof dish (trim the bottoms to enable this) brush with olive oil, and bake for 45 minutes or until tender.

Using a sharp knife, cut each pepper across into 4-6 slices and serve with Ratatouille (page 160) or Garlic Potatoes Corfu Style (page 156).

Mexican Tortillas with Garlic, Lime and Refried Beans

To make 4 lazy tortillas

90 g/3 ounces/3 heaped tbsp finely ground yellow polenta meal

20 g/1 ounce/1 heaped tbsp buckwheat flour

200 ml/generous 6 fluid oz/¾ cup water

Instructions

When cooked, these tortillas look just like the real thing—on one side only. On the other side they look like pancakes! Needless to say, hide the pancake side with your filling and no-one will notice the difference.

Mix the ingredients thoroughly. Depending on your flours, you may need a little more or a little less water, so don't be afraid to experiment a bit. Heat a dry non-stick frying pan over a medium to high heat. Stir the mixture then pour in a ladleful and gently shake the pan so that it quickly spreads out on all sides to the thickness of a pancake. Try to keep the shape circular, and aim to make the tortillas about 12 cm/6 inches in diameter.

After about one minute, when the top has set and the edges start to curl upwards, flip the tortilla over and cook the other side. Press down with a spatula and cook for another minute or until the bottom is looking slightly floury with brown specks.

Make the other three tortillas in the same way, and stack them, separated by a layer of absorbent kitchen paper, until you are ready to fill them.

What It's Good For

It would be very difficult to pack any more nutrients into a meal than you can get from this lovely dish. Here are just a few examples of what it provides. Beans and polenta flour: high-class protein combination. Tomatoes: anti-cancer carotene lycopene. Raw garlic: blood sterilizing, anti-candida and anti-cancer action. Onion: anti-allergy, anti-virus and anti-cancer flavonoid quercetin. Lime: vitamin C and blood vessel strengthening flavonoids.

To make the filling

450 g/1 lb/2 cups cooked
    pinto beans roughly
    mashed
4 fresh tomatoes, skinned
    and chopped
1 large onion, chopped
The flesh of 1 small lime,
    cut in four and sliced
Plus 1 tsp grated lime zest
2 green hot chilli peppers,
    cut into long, thin strips
4 cloves garlic, crushed
2 tbsp fresh coriander leaf
    (cilantro) chopped
2 tbsp extra virgin olive oil
1 tsp black mustard seeds
Tamari sauce
Low-sodium salt
Shredded iceberg lettuce
    and Garlic Crèmo (page
    206) to garnish

Instructions

Heat the olive oil over a medium heat in a deep frying pan (skillet), or preferably a stir-fry pan, and add the mustard seeds. When they begin to pop, add the chopped onion, 3½ cloves of the crushed garlic, and the chilli pepper strips.

Stir-fry until they are beginning to soften, then add the lime flesh and zest and fry for another two minutes, gently turning occasionally with a spoon without breaking up the lime pieces.

Fold in the chopped tomatoes and allow to cook for a further 2 minutes, occasionally turning the mixture, until the tomatoes are soft. Add the mashed beans, chopped coriander, the rest of the chopped garlic, a few dashes of tamari sauce and some low-sodium salt, fold in gently, turn down the heat to low and cover the pan. Leave for 5 minutes to heat through, occasionally turning the ingredients gently with a spoon. The beans will soften and blend with the other ingredients.

Meanwhile heat up the tortillas under the grill (broiler) and keep warm. When the filling is ready, hold a tortilla 'pancake side up' in your hand and pile filling into it, squeezing the sides slightly together. Cover the top of the exposed filling with a handful of shredded iceberg lettuce and pour over a few spoonfuls of Garlic Crème.

You can also make enchiladas by rolling the refried bean up in the lazy tortillas, laying the rolls seam-side down, and topping with a tomato, garlic and chilli sauce and a dollop of Garlic Crème.

Make a tomato salsa to go with either of these dishes, using finely chopped tomatoes, diced avocado, chilli pepper, coriander leaf and capers plus a squeeze of lemon juice and a dash of Tabasco chilli sauce.

Rejuvenation Soup (a one-pot meal)

Ingredients for 6 servings

1 organic chicken or duck carcass

The giblets (liver, neck and heart only)

1.7 litres/3 pints/6 cups water

Approx 200 g/7 ounces rice vermicelli

4 dark green cabbage leaves, shredded

2 carrots, sliced

2 tomatoes, roughly chopped

1 large onion, chopped

2 tbsp brown miso

Black pepper

Special Equipment

A pressure cooker

Instructions

You would normally use the remains of a roast chicken or duck for this soup, but any small bones will do, for instance those left after filleting a chicken.

Cut any greeny-yellow marks off the liver (these are bitter and come from bile). Put the bones in a pressure cooker with the giblets and water and press down on the carcass to ensure it is covered with water. Bring to full steam and cook for 45 minutes. Cool the pressure cooker in a sink of cold water until you can open the lid, then strain the stock through a sieve into a large saucepan. Dissolve the miso in the stock, season with black pepper and add the vegetables.

Once the contents of the sieve have cooled, use your hands to pick the remains of any meat off the neck and bones, and put them in the saucepan. Crumble the liver and thinly slice the heart, and put

What It's Good For

A great way to use the giblets from a chicken or duck, plus the bones which normally get thrown away. In effect, you are getting a couple more meals out of the bird. Liver is rich in vitamin A, folic acid, iron, copper, zinc and B vitamins. Bones are rich in calcium, magnesium and many other minerals, as well as glycine, which helps your liver to process toxins. Joint cartilage is rich in glucosamine, often sold as a supplement to help treat arthritis. Using this cooking method, cartilage from the carcass will dissolve in the liquid, providing as much glucosamine as taking supplements.

these in the pan too. Discard the remains of the carcass or feed to pets.

Now bring the pan to the boil and simmer for 30 minutes. Add the rice vermicelli and leave to soak in the soup for 2 minutes before stirring and serving. This soup makes a complete meal and can be refrigerated once cool and reheated as needed.

Plaice Meunière with Mustard, Lemon and Parsley Sauce

Ingredients for 2 servings

2 large plaice fillets

3 tbsp extra virgin olive oil plus 2 tbsp for frying

Juice of half a lemon

1 dessertspoon fresh or 1 tsp dried parsley, chopped

Gluten-free flour

½ tsp arrowroot powder

½ tsp yellow mustard powder

Low-sodium salt

Black pepper

This recipe works well with any flat fish fillets

Instructions

Combine the 3 tbsp oil in a small saucepan with the lemon juice and heat very gently. Blend the arrowroot and mustard powders with a tablespoon of water and stir into the mixture in the saucepan. Stir until it thickens, then remove from the heat and season with low-sodium salt and black pepper. Stir in the parsley.

Heat 2 tbsp oil in a frying pan. Season the plaice fillets and coat thoroughly with flour. When the oil is hot, put the fillet in the pan, skin side down. Cook for 2 minutes or until the bottom is beginning to crisp and turn golden, and the fish is almost cooked (it is cooked when it turns white). Turn over and cook the other side for 1 minute, pressing down a little with a spatula as the fish will curl up slightly. Drain the fish on absorbent kitchen paper and keep warm. Repeat with the other fillet if it did not fit in the same pan.

What It's Good For

Fish is not just an excellent source of good quality protein, but is easy to digest and contains little or no saturated fat. This makes it ideal for someone whose liver is under stress. Olive oil contains fatty acids which help to combat the yeast *Candida albicans*. Extra virgin olive oil is also now known to help preserve our mental powers as we age. Many people who find it hard to digest fats seem to have much less of a problem with olive oil.

When ready to serve, whisk the sauce, and pour over the fish. A good vegetable accompaniment would be Diced New Potatoes and Courgettes (see page 166), omitting the pesto coating.

Variation

This sauce can also be served with poached halibut.

Hot Spicy Prawns with Rice Noodles and Mixed Vegetables

Ingredients for 1 serving

115 g/4 ounces rice noodles

115 g/4 ounces/½ cup frozen mixed vegetables diced small (e.g. peas, carrots, peppers, [sweet]corn)

1 handful frozen peeled prawns (shrimps)

1 tsp tamari sauce or Thai fish sauce*

4 tbsp extra virgin olive oil

Low-sodium salt

Cayenne pepper

Special Equipment

A stir-fry pan

Instructions

Put the vegetables in a small lidded saucepan with 2 tbsp olive oil and heat gently until thawed. Continue cooking gently for 5 minutes, ensuring they do not dry out. Add a tablespoon of water if necessary. Remove from the heat, sprinkle with cayenne pepper and stir.

Follow the instructions on the rice noodles packet with regard to soaking them in hot water, although you may find that halving the soaking time indicated on the packet produces a better result (ideally they should still be definitely 'al dente' because stir-frying will finish cooking them). I like to use thin noodles—slightly thicker than vermicelli—which take only 2 minutes to soak.

As soon as the noodles have finished soaking, add some cold water to stop them cooking then drain them in a large sieve and leave the sieve over a bowl.

Heat a stir-fry pan over a medium heat.

What It's Good For

When cooked in this way, frozen vegetables are rich in vitamins and minerals. The vegetables are frozen soon after harvest and do not then lose nutrients like those which hang around in shops and then at home for several days. But if you defrost frozen vegetables and then throw away their defrost liquid, you will be throwing away most of their vitamins. Likewise if you boil them and then throw away the cooking water.

When hot, add 2 tbsp olive oil and then the prawns (shrimps). Stir-fry for about 20 seconds, then add the tamari sauce or fish sauce followed by the drained noodles, and stir-fry for another 20 seconds. By now the noodles should be soft. Add the cooked vegetables and stir-fry together briefly until thoroughly incorporated. Pile on to a plate and eat immediately.

Variations

Instead of prawns I often use fish fillets (salmon, whiting, haddock etc.) which can be poached in a few tablespoons of water in a lidded pan over a low heat for five minutes, then flaked and added with the cooked vegetables. My favourite variation is to use finely shredded green cabbage instead of frozen vegetables. Use a mandolin-type appliance to shred it, then briefly stir-fry it in olive oil in the stir-fry pan, add 2 tbsp water, cover the stir-fry pan tightly, and leave it over a low to medium heat to steam for 5 minutes. Stir the cabbage into the noodles as you did with the frozen vegetables.

You could also use small pieces of leftover steamed vegetables such as broccoli and carrots. Just add them to the noodles then put a lid over the stir-fry pan and leave to heat through for 2 minutes over the lowest possible heat before serving.

This is delicious and satisfying dish for the kind of person who often arrives home late, tired and hungry, and would rather order a take-away or pizza than start cooking. Now you will never need another take-away. Making this dish takes less time than waiting for your take-away, and costs a fraction of the amount.

Like other seafood, shrimps and prawns are rich in nutrients from the sea, including zinc and iodine.

Baked Salmon Parcels with Lime and Dill

Ingredients for each serving

One salmon fillet weighing about 115 g/4 ounces

Limes (one for each 3-4 fillets), thinly sliced

Olive oil

Fresh dill weed, roughly chopped

Low-sodium salt

Freshly ground black pepper

Instructions

Preheat the oven to gas mark 4

Brush the salmon fillets with olive oil then season with low-sodium salt and freshly ground black pepper. Sprinkle a pinch of chopped dill over the fish, then lay 3 overlapping slices of lime on top. Place each fillet carefully in the centre of a piece of baking foil, and fold the foil around the fish, tucking in the edges to make a parcel. If you wish to avoid aluminium, it is possible to make the parcels with baking parchment or grease-proof paper instead. Use a stapler to hold the edges of the parcel together. Lay the parcels in an open oven-proof dish or tray and bake in the oven for 20 minutes or until the fish is opaque throughout. Never overcook fish—it is at its best when only just done.

Serve immediately, with Sour Cream (page 205) and mixed vegetables, or with a Baked Rice dish (pages 152 and 153).

What It's Good For

Like herrings (see recipe on page 64), salmon is a so-called 'oily' fish, rich in omega 3 oils which help prevent red blood cells from clumping together and causing heart attacks. You may not know that these oily fish themselves are a far richer source of omega 3 oils than fish oil supplements. Salmon is also one of the few good sources of the powerful antioxidant astaxanthin.

Red Thai Curry with Pan-Fried Tofu

Ingredients for 1 serving

3 thick slices from a block of firm tofu

Half a can of coconut milk

½ cup mixed frozen vegetables (e.g. carrots and red sweet [bell] peppers diced small, peas, sweetcorn [corn])

1 portion uncooked vermicelli rice noodles or 1 portion cooked brown rice

150 ml/¼ pint/½ cup water

2 tbsp groundnut oil for frying

1 tbsp gluten-free flour

2 tsp red Thai curry paste (more if you like it stronger)

Low-sodium salt

Cayenne pepper

Instructions

Cut the tofu into bite-size pieces, pat dry with kitchen paper, sprinkle with low-sodium salt and cayenne pepper and coat well with flour. Heat the oil in a frying pan (skillet). When hot enough for the tofu to sizzle, carefully put the pieces in the pan and fry on each side for 1-2 minutes or until golden. Drain on absorbent kitchen paper.

Heat the water in a saucepan. Add the curry paste and coconut cream, stirring until dissolved. Add the frozen vegetables, put the lid on the saucepan and simmer for a few minutes.

Place the vermicelli rice noodles in a bowl. Boil a kettleful of water and pour the water generously over the noodles, leaving them plenty of room to swell. Leave for 2 minutes then run some cold water into the bowl before draining the noodles thoroughly in a large sieve. If using rice, heat the rice in a tightly lidded pan over a medium heat with 2 tablespoons of water. When the vegetables are heated through, stir in the fried tofu pieces and coat with the sauce. Serve the rice or noodles with the vegetables and tofu on top and the sauce spooned over.

What It's Good For

Tofu, with its richness of hormone-balancing compounds, and coconut milk— much healthier than other fats (see page 32), are key ingredients here, with mixed vegetables providing antioxidants, and cayenne pepper in the curry paste helping to warm the circulation and improve the digestion. This delicious meal can be put together in only 10 minutes.

Pasta Spirals Baked with a Sauce of Tomatoes Mushrooms and Olives Topped with Sour Cream

Ingredients for 4 servings

700 g/1½ lb/3 cups fresh tomatoes, skinned and chopped (you could also use good quality plum tomatoes canned in natural juice)

225 g/8 ounces/1 cup onions, finely chopped

225 g/8 ounces/4 handfuls pasta spirals made from rice or corn

225 g/8 ounces/1 cup mushrooms, finely diced

2 tbsp tomato purée (paste)

6 black olives, stoned and cut in four

(not ones preserved in lemon or vinegar)

4 cloves garlic, peeled and chopped

Instructions

Preheat the oven to 180°C/350°F/gas mark 4. In a large saucepan, gently fry the chopped onion in 4 tbsp olive oil until soft but not brown. Stir in the chopped garlic and cook for half a minute, then stir in the chopped tomatoes. Put a lid on the pan and cook over a medium heat for 15 minutes to break down the tomatoes. Fry the diced mushrooms in 3 tbsp olive oil until golden.

Remove the lid from the saucepan, add the tomato purée, mushrooms, olive pieces and low-sodium salt, and continue to boil for 45 minutes over a medium heat without the lid until the sauce is reduced to a thick consistency. Stir in the chopped basil.

Put the pasta spirals in a large pan of fast boiling water and cook according to the directions on the packet until they are

What It's Good For

There are lots of goodies in this recipes, including chromium and B vitamins from the mushrooms, anti-cancer lycopene from the tomatoes, soy in the Sour Cream, and methionine in the pasta spirals (if made from rice). Methionine is turned to glutathione in your liver, and used to help it detoxify pollutants. Extra virgin olive oil is useful in the treatment of candidiasis, and is now known to help you retain your brainpower in older age.

Extra virgin olive oil

1 tbsp fresh basil, chopped

1 tbsp fresh chives, chopped

Low-sodium salt

Freshly ground black pepper

just 'al dente'. Do not overcook them. Run some cold water into the pan as soon as they are ready, drain them, put them in an oven-proof dish, and thoroughly mix them with 2 tbsp olive oil. Add the pasta sauce and stir together.

Cover the dish and bake in the oven for 30 minutes. Serve with Sour Cream (see page 205) spooned on top and a sprinkling of chives.

Brown Beans in a Spicy Tomato Sauce with Creamed Potatoes

Ingredients for 4 servings

450 g/1 lb/2 cups cooked borlotti beans* (see page 48)

450 g/1 lb/2½ cups tomatoes, skinned and roughly chopped

4 cloves garlic, peeled and crushed

2 tbsp extra virgin olive oil

2 tbsp tomato purée (paste)

1 tbsp wheat-free miso

1 tsp porcini mushroom powder

Dried or fresh chopped herbs according to taste: thyme, parsley, tarragon, basil

Cayenne pepper

*Borlotti beans are mainly used in Italian cooking. They look a little like kidney beans but are fatter, with a rich brown colour when cooked. If you cannot find them, use red kidney beans instead.

Instructions

Heat the olive oil in a large saucepan over a medium heat, then add the tomatoes. Crush them with the back of a kitchen spoon until they begin to release their juice, then dissolve the miso in the juice. Add herbs, seasonings, cooked beans and porcini mushroom powder, stir to incorporate thoroughly, then put the lid on the pan and simmer gently for 1 hour, stirring occasionally.

At the end of this time, remove the lid. Break some of the beans up by roughly mashing them with a fork or potato masher. The beans should end up just covered by sauce, so if necessary turn up the heat to fast boil away any excess liquid.

Serve with Creamed Potatoes (next page) and a topping of Sour Cream (see page 205) or Garlic Crème (see page 206).

What It's Good For

A satisfying dish for a winter's evening. Beans are rich in protein. Miso is rich in B vitamins. Tomatoes, especially when cooked and concentrated, are loaded with the anti-cancer carotene known as lycopene. If you have any difficulty with digesting beans, try using the Digestive Tea on page 222 to accompany your meal.

To make the Creamed Potatoes

Allow one large floury potato for each serving

Cold-pressed sunflower oil (or soy cream)

Low-sodium salt

Freshly ground black pepper

Special Equipment

A potato press.

If you don't have one, you can use an ordinary potato masher, but make sure the potatoes are cooked until very soft and beginning to break apart.

It is easier to make good creamed potatoes if you use a potato press—a metal press shaped like a very large garlic press. Cooked potato chunks are pressed through it, and emerge mashed through tiny holes, which eliminates all lumps. Do not try to make creamed potatoes in a food processor—they will turn to glue.

Cut the potatoes into chunks and boil them in one inch of water until tender. Remove from the heat. Rinse the potato press and a large bowl under the hot tap to warm them so that they will not cool the potatoes too much. Wipe the bowl dry. Using a slotted spoon, remove a spoonful of potato pieces at a time and put them through the press into the bowl. Using a wooden spoon, stir a few tablespoons of sunflower oil and potato cooking water into the potatoes. Add the seasoning. Keep stirring in the hot water until you have the consistency you want.

Alternatively you could omit the oil, and add soy cream instead. Serve immediately.

What It's Good For

Potatoes are often thought of as a 'fattening' food, but in fact are not at all high in calories. A medium-sized potato provides only about 110 Calories.

It is the butter and sauces potatoes are served with, and the oil they are fried in which can make them fattening.

Potatoes are rich in potassium and also contain some protein and a little vitamin C.

German Erbsensuppe (pea soup) with Carrots and Miso
A one-pot meal

Ingredients for 4 servings

225 g/8 ounces/1 cup dried marrowfat peas

115 g/4 ounces/firm, low-fat sausage (optional) such as cabanos or chorizo, cut into large chunks

2 medium potatoes, diced

3 medium carrots, cut into chunks

1 large onion or 1 leek, cut into chunks

1 tbsp pale miso

Low-sodium salt

Freshly ground black pepper

Special Equipment

A pressure cooker

Instructions

Pour boiling water over the peas, allowing plenty of room for them to swell, and soak them overnight.

Discard the soaking water, then put the peas in a pressure cooker and cover with cold water. Bring up to full steam then cook for 5 minutes*. Plunge the pressure cooker into a sink of cold water to prevent further cooking and reduce the pressure enough to allow you to open the lid. The peas should be well-softened, and some of them quite mushy. If not, replace the lid on the pressure cooker, and repeat the process, cooking for a further two minutes, or as needed.

Stir in the miso then the vegetable and sausage pieces (if used). Pour in just enough water to cover the ingredients, stir well, then bring back to the boil and simmer over a low heat for one hour without pressure, stirring occasionally.

What It's Good For

Like beans, marrowfat peas are rich in protein, and this dish makes a substantial and highly nutritious complete meal. Sausages are mentioned as an optional ingredient because it is traditional to cook this dish with them. Some types are not particularly fatty and a little goes a long way.

But do remember that sausages and ham contain preservatives and often quite a lot of salt.

Season with low-sodium salt and freshly ground black pepper and serve in large shallow stew plates.

Variations

In Germany all types of vegetables are thrown into this soup and it is very good for using up leftovers. You can also cook it with yellow split peas instead of marrowfat peas, or, instead of sausage, add some lean chunks of cooked ham to heat through just before serving.

*Older peas may need longer cooking times

Curried White Beans with Aubergine and Tomato

Ingredients for 2-3 servings

3 handfuls cooked white haricot (navy) beans (see page 48)

1 small aubergine (eggplant), diced

1 medium potato, diced

2 large tomatoes, chopped

1 medium onion, chopped

2 cloves garlic, chopped

½ tsp chilli paste or 2 tsp red Thai curry paste

2 tbsp coconut oil

1 tsp fresh ginger, chopped

Low-sodium salt

Instructions

Using a stir-fry pan, fry the onion in the oil until it turns translucent, then stir in the chopped garlic and ginger, the curry paste and then the beans and stir-fry for half a minute.

Add the diced potatoes and aubergines and stir everything well together.

Stir in the chopped tomatoes and low-sodium salt. Add water to almost cover the ingredients in the pan.

Cover tightly and leave to simmer over a low heat for 20 minutes. Then turn up the heat to moderate and continue cooking with the lid off, stirring regularly to prevent the ingredients from sticking to the bottom of the pan, for another 20-25 minutes or until the sauce is well reduced and just coats the beans and potatoes.

Serve garnished with fresh coriander (cilantro), accompanied by brown rice or a piece of warm flatbread.

What It's Good For

Beans are a good source of B vitamins and protein, especially the amino acid lysine, which is lacking in most other plant foods. Aubergines—hailed in Ayurvedic medicine for their beneficial effects on female hormones—provide flavonoids and many vitamins and minerals. They are deliciously creamy although they contain no fat or oil. Tomatoes, especially when cooked, are a good source of lycopene, an anti-cancer carotene. Chilli peppers contain ingredients which help to relieve intestinal flatulence.

To vary the bland flavour of brown rice, try stir-frying it with a little olive oil and some chopped spring onion and garlic. Sprinkle in the herbs of your choice and a few dashes of tamari sauce or mushroom powder. It will become instantly delicious.

Pancake Pizza

Ingredients for 2 medium-sized pizzas

For the batter (dough)
55 g/2 ounces/1 tbsp fine oatmeal
55 g/2 ounces/1 tbsp spelt flour*
55 g/2 ounces/1½ tbsp soy flour
250 ml/9 fluid oz/1 cup water
1 rounded tsp baking powder

For the topping
Extra virgin olive oil
1 x 400 g can of chopped Italian plum tomatoes
110 g/4 ounces/1 cup grated hard goat or sheep's cheese

*See page 246

Instructions

Preheat the grill (broiler). Also preheat a lightly oiled frying pan over a medium-high heat. Put the tomatoes in a sieve over a bowl to drain off the liquid.

Mix the batter ingredients and beat until smooth. The batter has the right consistency if it settles into a round of about ½ cm/¼ inch in thickness when poured into the pan.

When the pan is hot, pour in half the batter and tilt a little if necessary to get a round shape. Cook for 1-2 minutes, or until the top of the pancake has set and the bottom is beginning to brown. Turn it over and cook the other side.

Put the cooked pancakes on an oiled baking sheet. Brush them liberally with olive oil, then spread with the chopped tomato flesh (and other topping ingredients if you wish). Cover well with the grated cheese then put under the grill

What It's Good For

This recipe is particularly useful for allergic children, since it is quite similar to real pizza, especially if you can find a really nice goat or sheep's cheese that grates well and melts nicely. The oatmeal in this recipe provides magnesium, and the tomatoes provide the anti-cancer carotene known as lycopene.

Protein is provided by the combination of the three types of flour and the cheese.

(broiler) to cook until golden and bubbling. Serve immediately.

Variation

Add some finely grated carrot and grated
goat or sheep's cheese to the pizza base
batter, make the pancake then cut it into
wedges and eat plain as a snack or accompaniment to a meal, or add toppings and
bake as above.

New England Real Baked Beans

Ingredients for 4 servings

450 g/1 lb/2 cups cooked
pinto* beans (see page 48)

4 tbsp tomato purée (paste)

4 tbsp blackstrap molasses

600 ml/1 pint/2 cups water
which has been saved after
steaming vegetables

4 bay leaves

Low-sodium salt

A pinch of cayenne pepper

*You could use white haricot
(navy) beans if you prefer.

Instructions

Preheat the oven to 140°C/275°F/gas mark 1.

Place the ingredients in a saucepan and bring to the boil, stirring well to dissolve the molasses. Transfer to a casserole dish and cover it tightly.

Place in the oven and cook for 4 hours. It will not spoil if left a couple of hours longer, though you should check occasionally to ensure that the beans are still covered with liquid.

Before serving, transfer the beans to a warm dish and fast-boil the sauce in a saucepan for a few minutes to concentrate it until it reaches your preferred consistency.

Serve the beans with Southern Sweet Potato Bread (see page 150) or with creamed potatoes (page 134).

What It's Good For

Beans are an excellent source of protein, especially when combined with grains (e.g. cornmeal, rice, oats, rye). They are also rich in B vitamins.

Blackstrap molasses is a thick residue left from sugar processing, and contains all the minerals of the sugar cane or sugar beet that were left behind when white or brown sugar was produced: calcium, magnesium, iron, zinc and manganese to name just a few.

Fillets of Red Mullet Fried Cajun-Style

Ingredients for 2 servings

4 red mullet fillets*

2 tsp paprika (not the hot variety)

2 tsp onion powder

2 tsp garlic powder

2 tsp dried thyme or oregano

1 tsp cayenne pepper

1 tsp ground black pepper

1 tsp low-sodium salt

Olive, coconut or groundnut oil for frying

*If your fishmonger does not sell them ready-filleted, ask him to fillet them for you.

Instructions

Using a mortar and pestle or a coffee grinder, grind the thyme or oregano to a powder, then mix thoroughly with the other dry ingredients. Spread the resulting powder out on a plate.

Dry the fish fillets with absorbent kitchen paper, then press both sides of them firmly into the powder until they are thickly coated.

Heat 4 tbsp oil in a frying pan over a high heat. When the oil is very hot, add the fish fillets, flesh side down, and cook for one minute. Turn over and cook the other side for half a minute, pressing down if necessary to prevent the fillets from curling up.

Drain briefly on absorbent kitchen paper then serve immediately with a vegetable or salad accompaniment. This dish goes very well with German Potato Salad (see page 176).

What It's Good For

Cajun cookery is hot and spicy and comes from New Orleans and other parts of the Southern United States. Cayenne pepper has two special benefits: it is warming and great for the circulation, and it also has a soothing effect on the digestive system, with the ability to combat intestinal flatulence.

Thyme and oregano contain antibacterial and antifungal ingredients and are useful as part of an anti-candida diet.

Queen Scallops with Rice Noodles and Spring Greens

Ingredients for 2 servings

225 g/8 ounces of queen
scallops* (excluding shells)
200 g/7 ounces spring (collard)
greens
200 g/7 ounces thin rice noodles
¼ pint/150 ml/½ cup cold
water
Olive oil
2 tbsp soy cream (optional)
1 tsp fresh parsley, chopped
1 rounded tsp pale miso
dissolved in ¼ pint/150 ml/
½ cup hot water
1 rounded tsp arrowroot
powder dissolved in 1 tbsp
water
Low-sodium salt
Freshly ground black pepper

* These are the very small
variety

Instructions

Trim and wash the greens. Cut them across into thick ribbons. Put a large stir-fry pan or saucepan over a medium heat. When hot add 2 tbsp olive oil and the greens. Stir well, then add the cold water and cover the pan. Turn the heat down to medium-low, cook for 5 minutes then season with low-sodium salt, stir and check that the water has not all evaporated. (If it has, add a little more). Replace the lid, cook for another 5 minutes then fast-boil away any remaining liquid. Remove from the heat; keep warm.

Bring a kettle of water to the boil then pour it over the rice noodles and leave to soak for 2 minutes. Drain then cover with cold water and drain again.

Put a frying pan over a medium heat; when hot add 2 tbsp olive oil. Briefly sear the scallops on either side in the hot oil and remove. Pour the miso and hot water into the pan, stir in the dissolved

What It's Good For

Greens are a member of the cabbage family, and contain ingredients which help your liver to break down pollutants in your body, helping to lower your cancer risk. Greens are rich in chlorophyll (which helps to neutralize toxins in your intestines), and in calcium, iron and lutein, a carotene type of antioxidant which has a protective effect on your eyesight. The calcium in green vegetables is easy to assimilate, making greens a better source of calcium than milk.

arrowroot, return the scallops to the pan and simmer for about 5 minutes. Stir in the parsley and soy cream and remove from the heat. Keep warm.

Heat 2 tbsp olive oil in a stir-fry pan over a high heat, then add the soaked rice noodles. Stir-fry for about 20 seconds then add the greens, combine gently and pour into a warm serving dish. Pour the scallops and their sauce on top, and use two forks to combine the scallops with the other ingredients. Season with black pepper and serve immediately.

Moroccan Couscous with Seven Vegetables

Ingredients for 2 servings

Millet grains measured up to the 120 ml/4 fluid oz/½ cup mark in a measuring jug

200 ml/7 fluid oz/generous ¾ cup water

1 cup of cooked chickpeas

½ cup raw cashew nuts, washed and drained

1 large courgette (zucchini) cut into chunks

1 medium onion, quartered

1 medium carrot, quartered

1 sweet (bell) pepper cut into 8 pieces

2 x 1 inch chunks of white mooli/daikon radish

4 chunks of pumpkin, squash, or vegetable marrow, each about 1 inch square

1 large tomato, sliced

2 tbsp olive oil

Instructions

Nowadays the grain product sold as couscous is usually made from crushed wheat, but traditional North African couscous can be made with millet grains. The grain is soaked and then cooked by steaming over a 'tagine', a meat and vegetable stew which imbues it with flavours. The simplified version here uses whole millet grains and omits the steaming process, but if you have a pan in which you can suspend a colander, or sieveful of cooked millet grains while the tagine cooks underneath, you could transfer the millet there to stay hot in the steam and absorb the flavours.

To cook the millet

Toast the millet grains in a dry frying pan over a medium heat for about 10 minutes or until they give off a roasted aroma and begin to change colour. Transfer them to a saucepan, add the water, cover, bring to the boil and simmer over a low heat for 30 minutes, ensuring they do not dry out.

Remove from the heat. Remove the lid,

What It's Good For

What a delicious way to get your daily vegetables. This dish is very versatile, and is a good way to use up any seasonal vegetables, especially white mooli/daikon radish, which is not a traditional vegetable in this dish, but is perfect for it. Radishes are said to balance the production of thyroid hormones, to dry up congestion and eliminate cold symptoms, and to stimulate the flow of bile, thus aiding digestion. Other traditional vegetables include quartered artichokes, white turnips

1 tsp turmeric

Cayenne pepper

Bouquet garni: a stick of
   celery tied up with
   parsley, thyme and
   rosemary

Spices: whole
   peppercorns, cloves,
   cinnamon and crushed
   cumin seeds tied up in
   muslin*

Low-sodium salt

Harissa (hot pepper)
   sauce to serve

*If you have trouble
finding muslin, you could
use a wire mesh 'tea
infuser' suspended in the
pan instead.

add 1 tbsp water, stir briefly, then replace the lid and leave undisturbed for five minutes. You can time the tagine to be ready now for serving with the millet, or transfer the millet to a colander set over the tagine as described above.

To make the tagine

Using a large saucepan with a heavy base, brown the onion and carrot pieces in the olive oil over a medium heat. Sprinkle with cayenne pepper. Next add the turmeric and all the other ingredients except the remaining herbs and spices. Stir together and pour in just enough water to cover them. Then add the bouquet garni and remaining spices.

Bring to the boil and simmer gently for 45 minutes. Using a slotted spoon, remove the vegetables from the pan and arrange them on top of the millet. Keep hot. Remove the bouquet garni and the muslin bag from the pan and reduce the sauce to about 300 ml/½ pint/1 cup by fast-boiling. Serve the sauce separately. Harissa, a fiery hot pepper sauce, is also traditionally served with couscous.

Variation

You could also add some chicken pieces to this dish. Just brown them at the same time as the onion, and proceed as before.

and green beans. Instead of cashew nuts you could use almonds, and instead of a tomato you could use an apricot. Millet is a very ancient grain and has been cultivated for longer than rice, wheat and rye. It is a rich source of many vitamins and minerals and is one of the best sources of the mineral silicon, which is needed for strong bones and teeth. People with food intolerances rarely have a problem with millet, as it is gluten free and easy to digest. It can safely be added to any hypoallergenic diet. Millet is also said to have anti-fungal properties and therefore may be able to help people with intestinal candidiasis.

Grilled Chicken Nuggets Marinated in Ginger and Garlic

Ingredients for each serving

One medium-sized chicken breast, boned and skinned

1 tbsp olive oil

2 tbsp tamari sauce

1 tsp fresh ginger, finely chopped

1 tsp fresh garlic, finely chopped

Instructions

Cut the chicken breast into strips about half an inch wide. Whisk together the other ingredients in a bowl large enough to hold all the chicken. Place the chicken in the bowl and ensure it is well coated with marinade.

Leave for several hours (preferably overnight), turning the chicken occasionally.

Remove the grid from the grill (broiler) pan. Line the pan with foil, then preheat the grill to its highest setting.

Roll up the chicken strips and thread them close together on a flat skewer. Lay the skewer over the grill pan and place under the hot grill.

Cook for about 5 minutes on each side or until the chicken is cooked through. Serve with salad in a piece of folded flatbread, or with rice or millet.

The remaining marinade can be poured over some cold, cooked rice or millet in a hot stir-fry pan. Simply toss and stir over a medium heat, with a little extra water if necessary, until the grains are heated through.

What It's Good For

Chicken is a good source of protein, and low in animal fat. While some therapeutic diets restrict protein, remember your liver cannot detoxify your blood unless it gets enough protein to manufacture essential enzymes. People with chronic fatigue syndrome especially need to avoid very low protein diets. When grilling meat and chicken, cut off and discard any charred, blackened pieces as they contain toxic compounds. Avoid barbecuing, because toxic smoke settles on the meat.

Side dishes and accompaniments

If you have children who won't eat vegetables, this could be simply because they don't like them boiled.

After all, most children like canned vegetable soups, so it could simply be a matter of how they're served.

Here are plenty of ideas for making them tasty and succulent—e.g. chopped small and baked with rice and onion, or made into a colourful rainbow salad.

Southern Sweet Potato Bread

Ingredients for 6-8 servings

1 medium-to large orange sweet potato, cooked and peeled

100 g/3½ ounces soy flour

100 g3½ ounces finely-ground yellow polenta meal

100 ml/3½ fluid oz soy or nut milk

2 tbsp sunflower oil

1 heaped tsp baking powder

Instructions

Preheat the oven to gas mark 5.

All sweet potatoes have a purplish skin. The only way to tell if the flesh is orange is to scrape one gently with a fingernail. When preparing for this recipe, leave the potato whole, prick it all over with a sharp knife or fork, then steam for about 45 minutes or until soft.

Roughly chop the cooked, peeled sweet potato and put it in a food processor with all the other ingredients. Using the blade attachment, whizz the mixture until smooth, then transfer it to a small oiled loaf tin and bake for 40 minutes or until beginning to brown on top.

Serve cut into hunks with New England Baked Beans (page 142) and other bean dishes.

What It's Good For

Both yellow polenta and sweet potatoes with orange-coloured flesh are rich in powerful antioxidants known as carotenes (similar to beta-carotene) and so can help to prevent cancer.

This delicious sweet moist bread is best served freshly made and warm. Any leftovers can be wrapped in foil once cold. Reheat in the foil in a moderate oven for 10 minutes.

Warm Salad of Grilled Vegetables with Lemon Zest

Ingredients for 4 servings

2 medium onions, cut in four

2 sweet (bell) peppers, one red one green, deseeded and cut in four

4 medium tomatoes, halved

1 lemon

1 green chilli pepper, deseeded and finely chopped

1 handful Greek olives (black)

2 tbsp capers

1 tbsp coriander leaves (cilantro), coarsely chopped

Extra-virgin olive oil

Instructions

Preheat the grill (broiler) to its highest setting.

Thread the onion quarters, sweet pepper pieces and tomato halves on skewers, brush liberally with olive oil and place under the grill (broiler) for 10 minutes, turning and brushing again with oil occasionally until the vegetables are beginning to tinge brown.

Meanwhile grate the zest off the lemon, then make a dressing by juicing the lemon and whisking the juice with 4 tbsp olive oil.

Add the zest to the dressing, together with the finely chopped chilli pepper and the capers.

When the vegetables are ready, slip them off the skewers, pour the dressing over them and ensure they are thoroughly coated.

Serve warm or tepid, sprinkled with the Greek olives and chopped coriander.

What It's Good For

One of the major cancer-fighting flavonoids found in onions is quercetin, which also helps to fight allergies and viruses and to prevent cataracts. Lemon peel has the flavonoid hesperidin, which fights varicose veins and fluid retention by preventing blood vessel walls from getting thin and leaky, and nobiletin, which is anti-inflammatory and helps the liver process toxins. Lemon juice and peppers are rich in vitamin C. Vitamin C is also needed for strong, healthy skin and blood vessels.

Baked Rice Dishes

Lemon Baked Rice

Ingredients for 4 servings

300 ml/½ pint/1 cup organic brown rice (pour the rice into a measuring jug to measure the quantity) soaked for 6 hours or more in 600 ml/1 pint/2 cups water

Half a fresh lemon (preferably unwaxed*)

2 medium onions thinly sliced into half-rings

1 handful sunflower seeds

8 tbsp extra virgin olive oil

Low-sodium salt

Black pepper

*If not unwaxed, scrub the lemon in very hot water with detergent to remove as much pesticide-treated wax as possible.

Instructions

Leaving the rice in its soaking water, bring to the boil in a lidded saucepan then simmer very gently for 20-25 minutes, until just tender. Quickly tip the rice into a large sieve to drain off any remaining water then tip the rice straight back in the pan, replace the lid and leave the rice undisturbed for at least 5 minutes.

Preheat the oven to 180°C/350°F/gas mark 4.

Heat the oil in a large frying pan or stir-fry pan and fry the onions over a high heat until they are beginning to turn golden and crispy. (You will probably need to do this in two batches to avoid over-crowding the pan, which will create too much steam.)

Cut the half lemon into four pieces and pick out all the pips. Whizz the lemon pieces in a food processor until finely chopped. Fold the cooked onions, chopped lemon and the sunflower seeds into the brown rice, and add the seasoning.

Put the rice in a casserole dish with a well-fitting lid, and bake for 40 minutes.

What It's Good For

This dish is very rich in cancer-fighting flavonoid antioxidants. One of the major flavonoids found in onions is quercetin, which reduces histamine and helps prevent cataracts. Lemon peel is rich in the flavonoid hesperidin, which fights varicose veins and fluid retention by preventing blood vessel walls from getting thin and leaky, and nobiletin, which has anti-inflammatory action and helps the liver to process toxins. Brown rice is an excellent source of B vitamins.

Walnut and Mushroom Baked Rice

Ingredients for 3-4 servings

In this recipe a cup is an ordinary teacup

2 cups cooked brown rice

1 medium carrot, grated

50 g/2 ounces/½ cup walnuts coarsely ground in food processor

1/4 lb mushrooms, diced

1 onion, cut in four

2 sticks celery, roughly cut into segments

1 green (bell) pepper, cut into 8 pieces

4 tbsp olive oil

A few leaves of fresh basil, chopped, or 1/2 tsp dried basil

Tamari sauce

Ground black pepper

Instructions

Preheat the oven to 180°C/350°F/gas mark 4.

Process the onion, celery and green pepper in a food processor until finely chopped. Place a large saucepan or stir-fry pan over a medium to high heat. When hot add 2 tbsp olive oil, then add the onion, celery and green pepper mixture and the grated carrot. Stir-fry for five minutes until the mixture begins to soften, then take off the heat. Transfer the contents to a bowl.

Clean and dry the pan then replace over a high heat and add the chopped mushrooms and oil. Stir-fry until beginning to turn golden brown.

Take off the heat, add back the vegetables to the pan, and mix in the chopped walnuts, basil, pepper and a few dashes of tamari sauce. Finally fold the grains in gently, ensuring that they do not break up.

Transfer the contents to a casserole dish with a well-fitting lid, and bake for 40 minutes.

Variations

Use cooked buckwheat or millet instead of brown rice, or include a tablespoon of wild rice.

What It's Good For

The combination of walnuts with brown rice in this recipe yields substantial amounts of protein, so this dish could just be served with a salad or a portion of braised vegetables, and perhaps some garlic mushrooms. It provides a very broad spread of nutrients, from B vitamins (brown rice) to beta carotene (carrots), chromium (mushrooms), and vitamin C (peppers). Other beneficial items include fluid retention-fighting coumarin (celery) and allergy-fighting quercetin (onions).

Vegetable Pakoras

Ingredients for 2 servings

1 medium waxy potato, cut in four

1 medium carrot, cut into several segments

1 medium courgette (zucchini), cut into several segments

3 tbsp coconut, groundnut or olive oil

2 tbsp gram (chickpea) flour

One teaspoon grated ginger

One teaspoon of curry powder

Instructions

Grate all the vegetable pieces together, using a food processor, or coarsely grate them by hand. Do not add any form of salt to the vegetables, as this will make them release liquid. Mix the vegetables with the gram flour, grated ginger and curry powder until well incorporated.

The vegetables must be cooked immediately as potatoes discolour quickly when grated.

Heat the oil in a large frying pan over a medium heat. Divide the mixture into four portions. Form two portions into a round shape with your hands. Put them in the frying pan, and gently flatten them, pressing with the edge of a spatula. (The edges can remain ragged.)

Cook the pakoras for 2 minutes until the edges are turning golden and crispy, then turn them over to cook the other side. Once cooked keep in a warm place until ready to serve. Repeat with the remaining portions.

What It's Good For

Taking only a few minutes to make, these succulent little pakoras are a delicious and unusual way to serve vegetables. Carrots are rich in antioxidant carotenes, especially beta carotene. Potatoes and courgettes are a good source of potassium and many vitamins and minerals.

Serve as a light snack with chutney or as a vegetable accompaniment, or cold as part of a buffet meal.

Garlic Potatoes Corfu Style

Ingredients for 4 servings

4 large potatoes, peeled

4 cloves of garlic, chopped

100 ml extra virgin olive oil

1 tsp chopped fresh rosemary

Boiling water

Low-sodium salt

Freshly ground black pepper

Instructions

Preheat the oven to 200°C/400°F/gas mark 6.

Cut the potatoes into large dice or thick slices and place in a shallow oven-proof dish. Sprinkle with seasoning, followed by chopped garlic and rosemary, then pour in the olive oil. Top up with enough boiling water to almost cover the potatoes, cover the dish with foil and place in the oven.

Cook for 45 minutes, then remove the foil and cook for a further 30 minutes uncovered, or until the water has evaporated and the potatoes are crisp and golden on top and tender in the middle. Drain off the excess oil, which is full of flavour and can be saved for another dish.

As the level of oil drops with the evaporation of the water, all the potatoes are coated with the oil and the wonderful flavours of the garlic and rosemary.

Variations

In Corfu, this dish is often made with a selection of different vegetables, e.g. courgettes (zucchini), carrots, onions and tomatoes.

What It's Good For

Eating this dish, you won't be able to help dreaming of sun-drenched Mediterranean shores! Potatoes are rich in potassium and minerals, and although only raw garlic has anti-bacterial and anti-fungal effects in the intestines, cooked garlic still has many beneficial effects on arteries, blood pressure, cholesterol, diabetes and the elimination of toxic (heavy) metals from the body.

Onion Marmalade

Ingredients for 3-4 servings

450 g/1 lb onions, peeled

2 tbsp extra virgin olive oil

Low-sodium salt

Instructions

Using a mandolin type appliance (with a spiked holder for the onions so that you don't slice into your fingers!) slice the onions thinly, then place them in a stir-fry pan with the oil over a medium heat. Using a large spoon, break up the onion slices into rings, and stir-fry until well-coated. Put a lid on the pan, and leave the onions to sweat over a very low heat for 30 minutes. Remove the lid, add low-sodium salt and stir-fry the onions with the lid off for 10 minutes to reduce any excess moisture. The onions should be soft and melting.

Reheat before serving. This is especially good with fish and steamed potatoes.

What It's Good For

The therapeutic value of the humble onion is often forgotten in favour of its famous cousin garlic. Onions are a rich source of the flavonoid quercetin, which is similar to the drug disodium chromoglycate, given to allergy sufferers to switch off their symptoms. Like the drug, quercetin inhibits the release of histamine, which is responsible for allergic symptoms and asthma attacks. Quercetin is also being researched for its anti-viral properties.

Polenta with Olives and Sun-Dried Tomatoes

Ingredients for 4-6 servings

250 g/9 ounces yellow polenta meal, preferably coarse-ground

1½ litres/2½ pints/5¼ cups boiling water

50 g/2 ounces/1 cup white mushrooms, diced small and fried for 2 minutes in 1 tbsp olive oil

8 large green olives, stoned and cut in four

15 g/½ ounce/1 heaped tbsp sun-dried tomatoes, thinly shredded

Olive oil for frying

Low-sodium salt

Freshly ground black pepper

Instructions

Pour the polenta meal and low-sodium salt into a saucepan containing the boiling water, whisking it rapidly as you do so to prevent lumps from forming. Turn the heat down to a gentle simmer and stir the polenta from time to time with a large wooden spoon, leaving the lid off the pan. Keep stirring until the mixture is gelatinous and stiff.

If there are directions on the polenta packet you can follow those instead.

When the polenta is ready, combine the diced mushrooms, olive pieces and sun-dried tomato shreds and fold them evenly and very gently into the polenta. Spoon the polenta into an oiled shallow dish large enough to result in a layer 1-2 cm/half to one inch thick when the polenta is spread out in it. Spoon in the polenta and then use the back of a fork to get the layer as even as possible.

Cover the dish with a kitchen towel

What It's Good For

Polenta is yellow cornmeal, rich in anti-cancer carotenes, and also essential polyunsaturated oils, vitamin E and complex carbohydrates.

Polenta cooked in this way is very versatile, and In Italy it is often used as a substitute for pasta.

and allow it to cool, then refrigerate until chilled. When you are ready to serve the polenta, divide it into portions, carefully remove them from the dish, and fry on each side in hot olive oil until golden and crispy. Serve with Ratatouille (see next recipe).

Ratatouille

Ingredients for 4 servings

1 medium-sized aubergine (eggplant) cut into large dice

1x400 g/14 ounce can of Italian plum tomatoes

2 medium-sized courgettes (zucchini) sliced about ½ cm/¼ inch thick

1 medium-sized green (bell) pepper, cut into about 20 pieces

4 cloves garlic, peeled and flattened with the side of a large knife

4 tbsp extra virgin olive oil

1 tsp mixed dried Mediterranean herbs (e.g. rosemary, oregano)

Low-sodium salt

Freshly ground black pepper

Instructions

Heat the oil in a large, heavy-bottomed saucepan over a medium heat. When hot, put all the vegetables in the pan. Stir, add the herbs and low-sodium salt, then cover the pan, bring to the boil, turn the heat down and sweat the vegetables over a low heat for one hour, stirring occasionally.

Remove the lid and check the consistency. If necessary, boil the ratatouille rapidly with the lid off to reduce the sauce until you have a thick consistency. The vegetables should not swim in liquid.

Stir in the freshly ground black pepper and serve hot or cold. This goes especially well with polenta (see previous recipe).

What It's Good For

This old southern French peasant dish could be one of the reasons why the Mediterranean peoples have a superior life expectancy. Rich in heart-disease preventing vitamin C and flavonoid and carotene antioxidants, this kind of food is just perfect for good body maintenance. Even the rosemary herb used in Provençale cookery contains antioxidants. I have recommended canned tomatoes here for their rich deep red, which indicates a good content of the anti-cancer carotene lycopene.

Baked Red Cabbage with Apple and Garlic

Ingredients for 4 servings

½ red cabbage, finely shredded

1 small, full-flavoured sweet apple, cored and thinly sliced

1 small onion, chopped

2 tbsp extra virgin olive oil

2 tbsp apple juice

1 tbsp raisins

2 cloves garlic, crushed or chopped

Black pepper

Instructions

Preheat the oven to 160°C/325°F/gas mark 3.

Heat the oil in a stir-fry pan or large, heavy-bottomed saucepan, and stir-fry the onion gently until softened.

Add the apple and garlic and then the shredded cabbage, stirring continuously until it has shrunk a little. Then remove from the heat, stir in the raisins, put the mixture in a casserole dish, pour over the apple juice, season with black pepper, cover tightly and cook for one hour.

Serve with roast organic chicken and Creamed Potatoes (page 134) or with a stuffed Potato Pancake (page 98).

What It's Good For

Members of the cabbage family are known to contain more anti-cancer substances than any other vegetables. And as a general rule, the more brightly-coloured a vegetable, the more free radical fighters it also contains in the form of flavonoids and carotenes. So, apart from being absolutely delicious, especially in this recipe, red cabbage is also extremely good for you! The red colour is anthocyanin, a flavonoid with powerful antioxidant action.

Cauliflower in Cream Sauce

Ingredients for 2-4 servings

425 ml, ¾ pint, 1½ cups boiling water

1 medium head of cauliflower

2 tbsp groundnut oil

1 rounded dessertspoon gluten-free flour

2 tbsp soy cream (optional)

Low-sodium salt

Special Equipment

A steaming basket

Instructions

Add the boiling water to a large saucepan which can be used for steaming. Divide the cauliflower into small florets. Wash thoroughly and place in a steaming basket inside the pan. Steam over a medium heat with the lid on for 15 minutes or until tender. Keep the cauliflower warm.

Put the oil in another saucepan over a gentle heat and stir in the flour. Drain the cauliflower cooking water into a jug, add some low-sodium salt, and whisk the hot cooking water gradually into the oil and rice flour mixture until evenly blended and thickened. Simmer over a low heat for 5 minutes, stirring from time to time. Add a little more water if the mixture is becoming too thick.

Add the soy cream and gently warm through without boiling. Pour the sauce over the cauliflower, toss so that it is well coated, and serve immediately.

What It's Good For

Like broccoli, cabbage and brussels sprouts, cauliflower belongs to the Brassica family of vegetables—famous for its ability to fight cancer-causing chemicals. The anti-cancer substances in these vegetables include indoles, phenols, coumarins and isothiocyanates. They provide raw materials for your liver to get rid of cancer-causing pollutants, and block the effects of cancer-causing compounds. They also help prevent many female problems, by assisting the liver to break down excess oestrogen.

Aromatic Carrots with Garlic and Shallots

Ingredients for 4 servings

4 medium carrots, cut into julienne strips

2 medium shallots, peeled and roughly diced

4 cloves garlic, peeled and crushed

2 tbsp extra virgin olive oil

A pinch of your favourite mixed dried herbs (e.g. tarragon and thyme)

Low-sodium salt

Freshly ground black pepper

Instructions

Heat the oil over a medium heat in a heavy-bottomed saucepan, and add the shallots. Cook until beginning to soften, then stir in the garlic and carrot strips. Ensure they are coated with oil.

Season with low-sodium salt and a sprinkling of herbs, then add four tbsp water, turn the heat down to its lowest setting, and cover the pan tightly. Cook for 25 minutes, adding a little more water if the pan looks like drying out.

If there are more than a couple of tablespoons of cooking juices in the bottom of the pan, turn up the heat to fast-boil it until reduced. Gently turn the carrots to moisten them with the juices, then season with freshly ground black pepper and serve immediately.

Variation

Try mixing the carrots with quartered brussels sprouts. This cooking method (braising) can also be used with shredded cabbage and dwarf green beans.

What It's Good For

This is a wonderful nutrient-conserving method of cooking carrots, and so delicious that you will never again want to cook them any other way. Carrots are rich in antioxidant carotenes, especially beta carotene. Because people who eat a lot of carrots get less lung cancer, scientists have carried out research giving beta carotene supplements to smokers to see whether supplements have the same effect. It appears that they are not nearly so effective as carrots themselves.

Crispy Potato Cakes

Ingredients

Allow 1 medium starchy potato for each serving of 2 potato cakes

Olive oil for frying

Low-sodium salt

Special Equipment

A round metal 'egg ring', 'cooking ring' or pastry cutter with a diameter of about 3 inches for each potato cake.

Instructions

Peel and coarsely grate the potatoes, putting the gratings into a bowl of cold water. Using your hands, remove handfuls of grated potato from the water, squeeze out the excess water and lay the grated potato on a clean tea towel. Fold the tea towel over and press the potatoes again to dry them as much as possible.

Put a large frying pan over a medium heat and coat the bottom with a thin layer of olive oil. When the oil is hot, put the cooking rings into the pan, and drop grated potato into each ring, pressing down gently so that you get a cake with a thickness of about ½ cm/¼ inch. Drizzle a teaspoon of olive oil over the potato cakes, then sprinkle with a pinch of low-sodium salt. Cook for five minutes, or until the bottom of the cakes is crisp and golden, then carefully remove the rings,

What It's Good For

Potatoes are rich in potassium and also contain some protein and a little vitamin C. They are often thought of as a 'fattening' food, but in fact are not at all high in calories. A medium-sized potato provides only about 110 Calories.

It is the butter and sauces potatoes are served with, and the oil they are fried in which can make them fattening. Shallow-frying in olive oil does increase the calorie content, but olive oil is one of the least harmful oils to cook with at the high temperatures of frying.

turn the cakes over and cook the other side without the ring.

Drain the cakes on absorbent kitchen paper and keep them warm while you cook the next batch. Serve with apple sauce or as a vegetable accompaniment.

Diced Fried New Potatoes and Courgettes with a Pesto Coating

Ingredients for 4 servings

4 medium-sized new potatoes, unpeeled, diced small

2 medium-sized courgettes (zucchini), diced

1 large handful fresh basil leaves

25 g/1 ounce/1 small handful walnuts or pine nuts

4 tbsp extra virgin olive oil, plus

Ordinary olive oil for frying

1 clove garlic

Low-sodium salt

Instructions

Put enough olive oil to form a ½ cm/ ¼-inch layer in a large frying pan over a medium to high heat. When hot, add the diced potatoes but do not overcrowd the pan. If necessary, cook them in two batches. Stir and turn over the potatoes occasionally to ensure that they cook as evenly as possible. When done, they should be golden and slightly crispy. This should take about 10 minutes. Remove the potatoes from the pan with a slotted spoon, drain them on absorbent kitchen paper and keep them warm.

Put the pan back over the heat and cook the diced courgettes in the same way, adding a little more oil if necessary. The courgettes should take about 5 minutes to cook. When done, remove them from the pan, drain them briefly on absorbent kitchen paper and keep warm.

Make the pesto coating by putting 4 tbsp olive oil in a blender with the garlic,

What It's Good For

In herbal medicine, basil was traditionally used against nervous irritability. It is little used by herbalists today. It also has anti-fungal, anti-bacterial and anti-parasitic properties, which are useful for people suffering from candidiasis and other imbalances in their intestinal bacteria. Walnuts are sometimes known as 'brain food', perhaps because they look like tiny brains! They are rich in essential polyunsaturated oils, protein, vitamin E, calcium, iron and zinc.

fresh basil, walnuts or pine nuts and low-sodium salt. Whizz until smooth and creamy.

Combine the potatoes and courgettes in a bowl and spoon in the pesto sauce. Fold together until the vegetables are thoroughly coated and serve immediately. This goes well with the Plaice Meunière recipe on page 126.

Braised Cornish Vegetables and Pasties

Ingredients for each serving

1 medium potato

1 piece of swede (rutabaga) the same size as the potato

Half a medium onion

1 tbsp extra virgin olive oil

Low-sodium salt

Pepper

Instructions

These vegetables are the traditional filling inside a Cornish pasty, minus the meat. They make a succulent and delicious vegetable accompaniment which I find extremely more-ish!

Finely dice all the vegetables, then sweat them over a very low heat in a lidded pan with the olive oil for 30 minutes, stirring occasionally and adding a tablespoon of water if they show any sign of sticking to the bottom of the pan. Serve with grilled fish or spiced bean röstis or roast organic chicken.

To make Cornish pasties, proceed as above, but cook for only 10 minutes. Drop spoonfuls of the mixture on to rounds of gluten-free pastry (pie crust) (see page 212), fold the pastry over the filling, brush the edges of the pastry with water, then seal the edges, make a small cut in the top for steam to escape, place on a baking tray and bake for 30 minutes at 190°C/375°F gas mark 5 or until golden.

What It's Good For

Swedes (known in Cornwall as turnips) are a sadly under-appreciated vegetable whose delicious sweetness perfectly complements potatoes and onions. Like cauliflower and cabbage, they are a member of the Brassica family which is famous for its anti-cancer benefits.

Vegetables with Garlic Crème on a Crispy Potato Base

Ingredients for 2 servings

2 Crispy Potato Cakes as
made on page 164

2 tbsp Garlic Crème (page 206)

4 tbsp vegetables, e.g.
braised onions and green
beans or the carrot dish on
page 163 or the warm
salad on page 151

Instructions

Spoon the warm Garlic Crème on to the potato cakes and top with the vegetables.

An elegant but simple dish, especially suited to a dinner party. You could serve this with most of the fish dishes in this book, or with chicken, stuffed peppers (page 120), Potato Ravioli (page 106) or Miniature Baked Omelettes (page 82). Just add a little green salad to garnish.

Variation

Use Hummus (page 79) instead of Garlic Crème.

What It's Good For

Many people, especially children, say they don't like vegetables. But maybe they just don't like them boiled? Who could resist the succulent sweetness of carrots cooked slowly with onions, garlic and olive oil, especially when combined with the sort of crispy potato dish that everyone seems to love? Sometimes children find vegetables too bland because they have a zinc deficiency and cannot taste them. If your child only seems to like very salty or very sweet food, this could be the reason.

Potato Gnocci (Italian potato dumplings)

Ingredients for about 40 small Gnocci (2 servings)

400 g/14 ounces/4 medium waxy potatoes*

50 g/1¾ ounces/2 tbsp potato flour (potato starch)

Low-sodium salt

*You must use waxy potatoes for this or the gnocci will not hold together when cooked. If unsure, choose varieties sold as 'salad' potatoes.

Special Equipment

A potato press

Instructions

Steam the potatoes in their jackets until tender (about 30 minutes). Hold them on a fork (so that you don't burn your fingers) and peel them with a small knife.

Put the potatoes through a potato press then work the potato flour into them using a fork. Once the two ingredients are evenly blended, change to a rubber spatula and mash to a paste. Turn the paste out on to a board or worktop, and knead the mixture, using your hands, until it is smooth and pliable. Divide in half.

Again using your hands, roll this dough into a long sausage shape with a diameter of about 1 cm/half an inch. Cut each roll into 10 segments, then briefly roll each segment between your hands to round it into an oval shape. Score the centre with the back of a fork to make little indentations which will help the gnocci to hold their sauce later on.

Put a large pan of salted water over a high heat and bring to the boil.

What It's Good For

Topped with tomato, mushroom and olive sauce (page 208) and a dollop of Garlic Crème (page 206). Folded gently into braised vegetables. Warmed through then coated with pesto sauce (page 166). Lightly coated with olive oil then sprinkled with a liberal topping of grated goat's or sheep's cheese and placed under a hot grill (broiler) until golden and bubbling.

As you prepare the gnocci, put them on a small plate then gently slide them off the plate into the gently boiling water.

These small gnocci should rise to the surface after about 40 seconds of boiling. After they have risen, count another 20 seconds, then remove them from the water with a slotted spoon. You can also make larger gnocci and they will take a little longer to rise.

South Indian Vegetable Curry (Sambar)

Ingredients for 2 servings

2 cups mixed vegetables* cut into 1 cm/½ inch pieces

1 large tomato, chopped

1 chilli pepper, deseeded, chopped

4 tbsp cooked red lentils**

2 tbsp olive oil

Low-sodium salt

Flavourings

A few dried curry leaves

1 tbsp chopped fresh coriander (cilantro) leaves

1 tsp turmeric

½ tsp each of black mustard, fenugreek and cumin seeds, ground cinnamon, coriander, asafoetida, black pepper, cayenne pepper

*E.g. potato, mooli/daikon radish, courgette, aubergine, green beans, onion, carrot.

**To cook red lentils, simmer in 2.5 times their volume of water for 25 minutes.

Instructions

1. Using a large saucepan with a heavy base, heat the oil and the seeds.
2. When the mustard seeds begin to pop, add the chopped chilli pepper, stir briefly.
3. Add all the vegetables except the tomato and stir-fry for 2 minutes.
4. Stir in the ground spices and turmeric.
5. Add 2 cups water and the chopped tomato, curry leaves and low-sodium salt.
6. Bring to a gentle simmer and cook for 30 minutes.
7. Stir in the cooked lentils and chopped fresh coriander (cilantro) and simmer for 5 more minutes.

Serve hot with rice. Sambar is traditionally a fiery dish. If you find it too spicy, cut down on the cayenne pepper or add it at the end to gauge how much you can tolerate.

What It's Good For

Sambar is a staple dish in South India. It can also be thinned with water and eaten as soup. Always fiery, sambar owes its heat to the chilli (cayenne) pepper, which has great health benefits, especially for the circulation. This is just the dish to eat if you feel a cold coming on. Chillies also stimulate the digestion and help to prevent flatulence.

Mini Rainbow Salads

Ingredients

Any combination of the following, depending on how many people you are catering for.

Finely grated swede (rutabaga)

Grated carrot

Grated raw beetroot or cooked beetroot cut into matchsticks

Tomatoes, thinly sliced

Grated mooli/daikon radish*

Sweet peppers (red, green, yellow) finely diced

*Long, white 'icicle' radishes

Special equipment

Cooking rings

Instructions

Pile layers of contrasting coloured ingredients into cooking rings, ending with a slice of tomato. Press down gently.

Transfer to a bed of lettuce or alfalfa sprouts (or a mixture of both) and spoon vinaigrette dressing (see page 218) flavoured with thinly sliced spring onion (scallion) over the top. Remove the rings and serve as soon as possible.

What It's Good For

I have extolled the virtues of the humble swede elsewhere in this book, but most people don't know that it is delicious eaten raw. I discovered this when I travelled to Iceland and was given a simple but exquisite dish of poached white fish with onions sweated in butter and a salad of grated raw swede and vinegar.

Raw grated carrot is good at preventing roundworm infestations so I put a little in my cats' food every day.

Millet with Crunchy Salad Vegetables and Fruit Pieces

Ingredients for 2 servings

Millet grains measured up to the 120 ml/4 fluid oz/ ½ cup mark in a measuring jug

200 ml/7 fluid oz/generous ¾ cup water

2 tbsp each of chopped, finely diced and/or grated salad vegetables: carrots, celery, sweet (bell) peppers, watercress, cucumber, mint, radishes, spring onion (scallion)

One apple or orange

4 tbsp vinaigrette dressing (see page 218)

1 tbsp lemon juice if using apple

Instructions

Toast the millet grains in a dry frying pan over a medium heat for about 10 minutes, or until they give off a roasted aroma and begin to change colour. Transfer them to a saucepan, add the water, bring to the boil and simmer over a low heat for 30 minutes.

Remove from the heat. Remove the lid, add 1 tbsp water, stir briefly, then replace the lid and leave undisturbed until cool.

Cut the apple into small dice, and place in a bowl of water with the lemon juice (to prevent discolouring).

Alternatively, if using an orange, cut into segments as described on page 185.

Shortly before serving, fluff up the millet with a fork, whisk the vinaigrette and stir it into the millet with the vegetables. Finally fold in the fruit pieces. This dish is excellent in a packed lunch.

Variation

You could use cooked brown rice or buckwheat instead of millet.

What It's Good For

Millet is a very ancient grain, and has been cultivated for longer than rice, wheat and rye. It is a rich source of many vitamins and minerals and is one of the best sources of the mineral silica, which is needed for strong bones and teeth. People with food intolerances rarely have a problem with millet, as it is gluten free and easy to digest. Millet is also said to have anti-fungal properties and therefore may be able to help people with intestinal candiasis.

Three-Bean Salad

Ingredients for each serving

2 tbsp cooked chickpeas

2 tbsp cooked red kidney beans

2 tbsp cooked black-eyed beans

1 spring onion (scallion), thinly sliced

1 stick celery, sliced

1 tbsp fresh chopped parsley

Half a green pepper, thinly sliced

Half a red sweet (bell) pepper, thinly sliced

2 tbsp vinaigrette dressing (see page 218)

Low-sodium salt

Freshly ground black pepper

Instructions

Combine all the ingredients and stir again just before serving.

This salad is ideal as part of a packed lunch together with German Potato Salad (page 176) and cold Falafel (page 94).

The dressing is best added when the beans are freshly cooked and still warm. If using canned beans, boil them for a few minutes in a pan of water, then drain. This helps the beans absorb more flavour from the dressing.

What It's Good For

Beans are rich in protein, filling, and delicious in salads. They are ideal in packed lunches because they contain a type of dietary fibre which slows down your absorption of carbohydrate from your meal. This helps to keep you feeling full for longer.

Sweet peppers are rich in vitamin C, and raw onion has some of the anti-fungal and anti-bacterial properties of raw garlic.

German Potato Salad

Ingredients for 4 servings

1 kg/2 pounds waxy potatoes

4 spring onions (scallions) finely sliced

6 tbsp extra virgin olive oil

4 tbsp mayonnaise (see page 210)

3 tbsp additive-free cider vinegar or white wine vinegar

1 tbsp capers, chopped

Low-sodium salt

Freshly-ground black pepper

Instructions

Steam the potatoes whole in their jackets until just tender (about 20-40 minutes depending on size).

Whisk together the oil, vinegar, salt and pepper in a large bowl, then stir in the spring onion slices and chopped capers. Leave to one side for the flavours to blend together.

When the potatoes are cooked, hold them on a fork (so that you don't burn your fingers) and peel them with a small knife.

Once peeled, cut into medium-sized dice and, while still warm, put them them in the bowl containing the oil and vinegar dressing. (Whisk it again first if it has separated).

Gently turn the potatoes in the dressing until they are well coated. Leave to one side for at least one hour so that the potatoes can absorb the dressing.

Just before you are ready to serve the potato salad, spoon in the mayonnaise and turn the potatoes around in it gently until they are evenly coated.

What It's Good For

Potatoes gain a delicious flavour by soaking up vinaigrette and then only need a light coating of mayonnaise. Sometimes anti-candida diets forbid vinegar because it contains yeasts and most Candida sufferers have a yeast allergy. However, those in vinegar (and miso) are natural yeasts, and are much less likely to cause allergic reactions than the commercial yeasts found in wine, beer, bread, pizza dough etc. If it does, use lemon or lime juice instead.

Super sweets

I guarantee you will be amazed at how easy it is to make delicious sweet dishes without sugar.

Those who try to sell us sugar insist there's no difference between the stuff in packets and the natural sugars in fruits. As far as your body is concerned, this is not true. Sugar bound up with the dietary fibre in fruit is absorbed much more slowly into your blood than added sugar, resulting in a more gradual rise in the hormone insulin.

But packet sugar can produce high insulin levels in your body very quickly. Too much insulin encourages fatty deposits on artery walls and slows down the body's ability to burn off body fat.

Fructose, which is one of the components of packet sugar and is the main ingredient of honey and agave nectar, cannot be turned into energy by the body, and is laid down as fat around our internal organs, causing the well-known 'apple shape' that doctors warn us about.

Artificial sweeteners have been shown to have a similar insulin-raising effect to packet sugar.

Little Castagnacci (Italian chestnut cakes)

Ingredients to make 12

200 g/7 ounces/1 cup chestnut flour

260 ml/scant ½ pint/1 cup water

Extra virgin olive oil

40g raisins

40g washed and dried brazil nuts, roughly chopped

1 tbsp fresh rosemary, chopped

Instructions

Preheat the oven to 190°C/375°F/gas mark 5.

Stir the water into the chestnut flour a little at a time until you have a smooth paste with a 'soft dropping' consistency. Stir in the raisins and chopped brazil nuts, and 2 tbsp olive oil. Drop a teaspoon of olive oil into each of the wells of a well-oiled shallow bun or muffin tin, followed by tablespoons of the chestnut mixture to a depth of no more than half an inch. Smooth the tops flat with a fork, then sprinkle on a little chopped rosemary and olive oil. Bake for 25 minutes or until cracked on top, then allow to cool for at least 30 minutes before serving. These cakes do not keep well and are best eaten within a day or two.

Variation

This recipe is best made with chestnut flour, but it is possible to make something similar with boiled, peeled, canned or vacuum-packed chestnuts. Blend the chestnuts in a food processor with enough water to achieve a slightly stiff consistency before adding the other ingredients.

What It's Good For

This is an adaptation of an ancient Italian recipe—crunchy on the outside, sweet and moist in the centre. Chestnut flour is available from health food stores or online. Selenium-rich brazil nuts can help to prevent heart attacks and cancer, and protect you against many pollutants. Always rinse and dry brazil nuts before use, as they are prone to develop mould soon after shelling. Chestnuts are low in oil, and rich in potassium, magnesium and iron. They are nutritionally similar to grains.

Chewy Chocolate Truffles

Ingredients to make 15 truffles

115 g/4 ounces dried dates

40 g/1½ ounces cocoa powder

55 g/2 ounces coarsely-chopped nuts

Instructions

Put the dates in a small saucepan, add just enough water to cover them and bring to the boil. Simmer on the lowest heat with the lid on for 15 minutes or until soft, then transfer the dates to a bowl.

Stir in some of the cocoa powder and mash it into the dates with the back of a tablespoon. Repeat until most of the cocoa powder has been incorporated, and you have a stiff, dough-like consistency. Tip half the chopped nuts plus the remaining cocoa powder on to a board, scrape out the dough and add it to them, then, using your hands, knead these remaining ingredients into the dough.

Roll the dough into a long sausage about 1 cm/half an inch or less in diameter, and cut it into 15 segments. (If necessary dust with more cocoa powder to prevent it sticking to the board.) Using your hands, roll each segment into a ball, flatten slightly, place in a fondant case and sprinkle with more chopped nuts.

Alternatively, make a slightly stickier mixture (using less cocoa powder), and roll the truffle balls in the chopped nuts so that they cling to them.

What It's Good For

Chocaholics will love this recipe, which contains none of the fat and sugar which makes overindulgence in ordinary chocolate so harmful. Cocoa powder is rich in iron and magnesium. Dates provide good quality dietary fibre, so these truffles can even help to keep your bowels working smoothly!

Gourmet Marzipan

Makes enough to cover 2 standard-size fruit cakes or to make 48 bouchées (mouth-size nibbles)

115 g/4 ounces dried dates

300 g/10½ ounces ground almonds/almond flour*

½ tsp natural vanilla essence

*For this recipe, commercially ground almonds produce a smoother result than those home-ground in a food processor.

Instructions

Put the dates in a small saucepan, add just enough water to cover them and bring to the boil. Simmer on the lowest heat with the lid on for 15 minutes or until soft. Transfer the dates to a bowl. Stir in the vanilla essence and some of the ground almonds. Mash them into the dates with the back of a tablespoon. Repeat until you have a stiff, dough-like consistency. Tip the remaining ground almonds on to a board, add the dough, then, using your hands, knead the remaining ground almonds into the dough.

The dough can be rolled out to the required dimensions for a cake (use more ground almonds to prevent the dough sticking to the board). First spread the cake with all-fruit apricot or cherry spread to hold the marzipan in place.

To make mouth-sized marzipan balls, roll the dough into sausages, cut off bite-size portions, and roll these into balls. These bouchées are delicious as they are or can be

What It's Good For

Dates are an excellent source of good quality dietary fibre, so this wonderful marzipan can even help to keep your bowels working smoothly. Do not consume marzipan or any nut-rich recipes if you suffer from herpes, since nuts are rich in arginine, an amino acid which can cause flare-ups of the herpes virus. On the other hand arginine is very good for high blood pressure. Almonds are rich in calcium and magnesium and are a good source of protein.

used to stuff prunes or dipped in melted bitter chocolate (with the aid of toothpicks to grip them). Place in fondant cases

Variation

Use unsulphured (dark brown) dried apricots instead of dates.

Baked Rice Pudding with Coconut Cream

Ingredients for 4-6 servings

115 g/4 ounces/scant 1 cup unpolished sweet rice which has been soaked in water overnight then drained

1 litre carton soy or nut milk

1 knob creamed coconut

1 handful raisins

2 tbsp almonds or cashew nuts, rinsed, dried and finely chopped

Use cashew nuts instead of almonds if you prefer a sweeter flavour.

Instructions

Preheat the oven to 175°C/325°F/gas mark 3.

Place the ingredients in a saucepan and bring to a gentle simmer, stirring until the creamed coconut has dissolved. Pour into a casserole dish placed on a baking tray, cover and bake in the oven for 2 hours. Check that the pudding does not boil over, and if necessary turn the heat down a fraction to prevent this. Remove the pudding after one hour to give it a good stir then replace it in the oven to finish cooking. You could also try cooking this in a saucepan on top of the stove if you wish, with the gas or electric ring on its lowest setting, and a heat diffuser under the pan if necessary. In this case a cast-iron enamelled pan would be best.

What It's Good For

Sweet rice is also known as glutinous rice, and is an ingredient in many oriental sweet dishes. Unpolished sweet rice (a form of brown rice) is available from health food stores. Creamed coconut contains coconut oil, which is not processed by the body like other fats and is good for people with post-viral chronic fatigue as it is rich in the anti-viral substance lauric acid.

Serve hot or cold

- On its own as a delicious breakfast dish, perhaps with prunes,
- Or as a dessert on a shallow plate beside one of the following garnishes:
  - Sliced sharon fruit (persimmon) or banana.
  - Reconstituted Hunza apricots (small dried apricots which are pale and very sweet in flavour).
  - A small chestnut cake (page 178).

Kiwi Fruit Slices in Apple Jelly with Strawberry Coulis

Ingredients for 4 servings

6 kiwi fruit, peeled and thinly
sliced

200 g/½ lb/1½ cups sweet
strawberries, chopped

275 ml/½ pint/1 cup apple
juice plus 2 tbsp

1 rounded tbsp agar flakes*

*If possible, a brand which
advertises that it
manufactures the agar using
traditional methods

Instructions

Sprinkle the agar flakes on the apple juice in a saucepan. Do not stir. Place the pan over a medium heat and bring to a gentle simmer. Simmer for 3-5 minutes, stirring occasionally until dissolved.

Arrange the kiwi fruit as evenly as possible in overlapping layers in a shallow serving dish, saving the prettiest slices for the top layer. You could also place them in individual dishes or moulds. (First line the moulds with cling film to help you turn out the jellies without breaking.)

Spoon the apple juice gently over the fruit, until it is just covered with jelly. Sets quickly (about 30 minutes). Refrigerate once cool.

To make the coulis, place the chopped strawberries in a blender with 2 tbsp apple juice and whizz until smooth. Serve with the jelly and a dollop of sheep or soy yoghurt.

What It's Good For

Kiwi fruit is one of the richest known sources of vitamin C. It is very pretty when sliced. Agar is a flavourless natural gelling and thickening agent made from seaweed. While many brands of agar (or agar-agar) are available in oriental shops, some are made by methods involving chemical extraction and bleaching. Macrobiotic agar is made by a traditional process. Agar can be used in jellies and aspics, and as a thickener.

Banana Crème

Ingredients for 2 servings

1 banana

100 g/3½ ounces/½ cup firm silken tofu

100 ml/3½ fluid oz soy or nut milk

55 g/2 ounces/½ cup raw cashew nut pieces, rinsed and dried

1 tbsp tahini (sesame paste)

2 tsp lemon juice

1 tsp natural vanilla extract

Instructions

Whizz all the ingredients except the tahini in a food processor using the S blade, until they are well blended, then add the tahini and continue to whizz until the mixture is very smooth. (This could take up to 5 minutes processing).

Serve the Banana Crème on its own in small glass dishes, topped with peeled orange segments, or as a topping poured over pear slices or a banana cut in half lengthwise. Decorate with a sliced strawberry.

To peel orange segments

Cut the ends off a whole orange. Stand it up then cut the peel off in a downward direction, working all the way around the orange and removing the outer white pith and membrane as you cut.

Using the same knife, cut between each segment, on either side of the membrane separating it from the next segment. Go all the way around the orange like this. The V-shaped orange pieces should easily come out perfectly skinned.

What It's Good For

Soy milk and tofu provide hormone-balancing isoflavones which help to prevent problems from excess or insufficient oestrogen, and excess testosterone: menopausal hot flushes, breast cancer, prostate cancer. Cashew nuts are low in oil and rich in potassium and magnesium, iron and zinc. Raw cashews are liable to develop a little mould while in their packets, so should be rinsed and dried before use. Bananas are rich in many vitamins and minerals, especially potassium.

Apple Custard

Ingredients for 2 servings

150 ml/¼ pint/½ cup soy or nut milk

4 tbsp apple sauce made as described on page 207

Instructions

Put the apple sauce in a small saucepan over a medium heat and whisk in the soy or nut milk. Keep whisking until the mixture thickens to the consistency of a thin custard.

What It's Good For

Apple peel contains amazing nutritional value. It is rich in quercetin and also pectin—a type of soluble dietary fibre. Pectin is used to set jam and is the reason why apple sauce can thicken soy or nut milk in this recipe. Pectin can also help to treat constipation, and it binds to toxins in your intestines and helps your body eliminate them. Unfortunately, although the skin is the most nutritious part of the apple, it is also the part most liable to contain pesticides, so try to use organic apples if you can.

Oat and Treacle Wedges

Ingredients for 8 servings

115 g/4 ounces/generous 1 cup rolled oats

55 g/2 ounces/scant half cup sunflower seeds

55 g/2 ounces/half cup raisins

50 ml/2 fluid oz/4 tbsp groundnut oil

2 tbsp date purée made as described on page 179

1 tbsp blackstrap molasses

Instructions

Preheat the oven to 180°C/350°F/gas mark 4.

Mix the dry ingredients in a bowl. Warm the date purée in a saucepan then stir in the molasses and oil.

Add the dry ingredients to the saucepan and stir until thoroughly incorporated.

Press the mixture evenly into an oiled 19 cm/7½ inch diameter sandwich tin and bake in the centre of the oven for 25-30 minutes.

Cut into 8 wedges while still warm and allow to cool completely before eating.

What It's Good For

Oats and dates are a great source of soluble dietary fibre which helps you excrete cholesterol. Oats are also rich in B vitamins, and are one of the best sources of magnesium. Blackstrap molasses is a thick residue left from sugar processing, and contains all the minerals left behind when white or brown sugar is produced: calcium, magnesium, iron, zinc and manganese to name just a few. Sunflower seeds are also rich in magnesium, as well as essential polyunsaturated oils.

Fruity Almond Cookies

Ingredients for 20 cookies

115 g/4 oz unsulphured dried apricots

110 g/4 oz ground almonds

50 g/4 oz soy flour

50 g/2 oz chopped mixed nuts

50 g/2 oz mixed dried fruit with peel

1 level teaspoon baking powder

1 teaspoon natural vanilla extract

Water as required.

Instructions

Preheat the oven to 180°C/350°F/gas mark 4.

Lightly oil a baking sheet. Dice the dried apricots, place them in a small saucepan and just cover with water. Bring to the boil and simmer very gently for 30 minutes. Add a little more water if necessary to prevent them drying out. Mix the dry ingredients together.

Once the apricots are cooked, purée them with a hand blender, adding a little more water if necessary to obtain a thick, smooth purée. Stir in the vanilla essence, then mix into the dry ingredients. Incorporate thoroughly, to achieve a thick, stiff paste.

Roll the paste into two long sausage shapes. Divide each roll into 10 segments. Roll each segment into a ball with your hands, press your hands together to flatten it, and place it on the baking sheet.

Bake in the preheated oven for 20 minutes. The cookies become stale after 24 hours but can be restored by gently warming in the oven.

What It's Good For

Dried apricots are orange in colour if treated with sulphur dioxide. This additive is an intestinal irritant and can cause bloating and gas. Unsulphured apricots (from health food stores) are dark brown and sweet. Apricots provide cancer-preventing carotenes, potassium and other minerals. Almonds are a great source of calcium and magnesium, iron, zinc and vitamin E and essential polyunsaturated oils. Due to their arginine content nuts are best avoided by people prone to cold sores and herpes.

Apple and Orange Mini-Muffins

Ingredients for 24 mini-muffins

175g/6 ounces/1 generous cup of fine maize flour (cornmeal) or fine yellow polenta flour

55g/2ounces/¼ cup soy flour

2 large sweet eating apples

150 ml/¼ pint/½ cup sweet Florida orange juice

150 ml/¼ pint/½ cup sunflower oil

1 teaspoon baking powder

a few drops of natural vanilla extract or a pinch of cinnamon

Special equipment

2 mini-muffin tins with 12 wells each, lightly oiled

Instructions

Preheat the oven to 180°C/350°F/gas mark 4.

Sift the dry ingredients into a bowl twice, to get as much air into them as possible.

Combine the liquid ingredients, then grate the apples into them. Stir, then pour the liquid into the dry ingredients and fold gently together until well combined. It is important not to use a mixer or to beat vigorously since this will reduce the air in the mixture.

Using a teaspoon, transfer the mixture to the wells of the mini-muffin tins and place on the middle shelf of the oven. Bake for 30 minutes or until a knife inserted into the muffins comes out clean.

This is a very adaptable recipe. You could experiment with adding chopped nuts, dried fruit, poppy seeds or other flavourings. You could also bake the mixture in a shallow cake tin and cut the resulting cake into squares to serve as a dessert with soy custard. For added sweetness and an unusual flavour, soak a piece of liquorice root in the orange juice for a few hours. Remove the liquorice before adding the juice to the mixture.

What It's Good For

Made only with fruit, unrefined flours and sunflower oil, you would not believe that these mini-muffins could taste so good and so sweet. Polenta is made from yellow corn, and is a good source of lutein and zeaxanthin, two nutrients that have special health benefits for the eyes.

Exotic Warm Fruit Salad in Grape Juice

Ingredients for 4 servings

1 peach, thinly sliced

1 small mango, skinned and chopped

1 kiwi fruit, peeled and sliced

2 slices fresh pineapple (or canned pineapple in juice, drained)

2 tbsp fresh or frozen (defrosted) blueberries

2 tbsp red grape juice

Instructions

Preheat the oven to 180°C/350°F/gas mark 4.

Place the fruits in an oven-proof dish, pour the grape juice over them and cover with a well-fitting lid. Cook in the oven for 15-20 minutes then serve immediately.

Recipe by Carolyn Gibbs

What It's Good For

Vitamin C and cancer-preventing flavonoid antioxidants are the outstanding nutrients found in fruit. Flavonoids also help to keep the walls of blood vessels firm, so that they are less likely to leak water into the spaces between your cells, causing fluid retention. Like all yellow or orange fruits, peaches and mangos also contain carotenes. Fresh pineapple contains bromelain, an enzyme which can aid digestion by breaking down protein.

Blueberry and Apple Crispy Pancakes

Ingredients for 8-10 small pancakes

1 large sweet dessert apple*

115 g/4 ounces/4 tbsp fresh or frozen (defrosted) blueberries or bilberries

55 g/2 ounce chickpea (gram) flour, sieved

25 g/1 ounce ground almonds (almond flour) or ground sesame seeds

75 ml/2¼ fluid oz/5 tbsp apple juice

Groundnut oil

*Choose a variety with plenty of flavour, such as Cox's, Royal Gala, Braeburn or Worcester

Instructions

Combine the chickpea flour, ground almonds and cinnamon. Slowly add the apple juice, stirring all the time. beat with a wooden spoon until smooth. Grate the apple (including the skin) and add to the batter together with the blueberries. Stir well.

Place a heavy-bottomed frying pan over a low to medium heat and add 2 tbsp oil. Once the oil is hot, drop dessertspoons of the batter into the pan, smooth down with a fork, and cook slowly until the bottom of the pancake has browned.

Flip over with a spatula and cook the other side. Re-oil the pan between batches. Serve immediately, with Coconut and Cashew Cream (see page 193) or Banana Crème (see page 185) and garnished with a few slices of fresh fruit such as oranges, pears or mangoes.

Variation

Use diced fresh pear and sliced banana instead of blueberries, and crushed or ground cardamom instead of cinnamon.

Recipe by Carolyn Gibbs

What It's Good For

This recipe provides high quality protein from the combination of ground almonds and chick pea flour, flavonoid antioxidants from the skins of the apple and blueberries, and buckets of vitamins and minerals. It is a common belief that we should not eat anything fried, and it is probably a good idea to stay off deep-fried foods, but in fact we do need to have some oil in our diet. The small amounts used in this book will ensure that you get that oil and are no cause for concern.

Black Forest Gelled Fruits

Ingredients for 4 servings

350 g/12 ounces frozen 'Black Forest' fruits*

150 ml/5 fluid oz/¾ cup red grape juice measured out, plus extra as required

15 g/½ ounce/1 rounded tbsp powdered gelatine or equivalent vegetarian gelling agent

*E.g. a mixture of blueberries, black cherries, blackberries, black grapes, strawberries, blackcurrants. This type of mixture is sold under various names in large supermarkets. You could also use the equivalent in fresh fruit.

Instructions

Place the fruit in a saucepan over a medium heat with the lid on and cook for about 3 minutes or until the fruits have softened a little and released some of their juice (if frozen, they do not have to defrost completely).

Remove from the heat. Put the 150 ml grape juice in a small saucepan and bring it to the boil. Take the pan off the heat and sprinkle the gelatine into it, whisking briskly until all the gelatine has dissolved.

Pour the fruit, with its juice, into a measuring jug. Add the dissolved gelatine and then top up with cold red grape juice to the 570 ml/1 pint/2 cup mark. Stir well.

Pour the mixture into a glass dish or mould and refrigerate until set (about two hours). Serve with Coconut and Cashew Cream (see page 193).

Recipe by Carolyn Gibbs

What It's Good For

The berries in this recipe contain a good mix of flavonoids. Flavonoids are the colourful pigments in their skins. The red and blue pigments are known as anthocyanins. Other flavonoids include catechins (found in grape seeds, cocoa powder and red wine) and quercetin (found in apple skins and onions). The medicinal actions of many herbs and plants (for instance Ginkgo biloba) are now known to be due to their flavonoids. Flavonoids can also help keep blood vessel walls healthy.

Coconut and Cashew Cream

Ingredients for 4 servings

1 small can coconut milk (165 ml/5.6 fluid oz)

85 g/3 ounces/raw cashew nuts, rinsed and dried

Instructions

Warm the coconut milk by putting the unopened can in a small saucepan of hot water for 10 minutes.

Open the can and put the coconut milk and cashews into a blender. Whizz until smooth and creamy, scraping the sides down occasionally with a rubber spatula. This process may take several minutes.

Set aside for one hour to thicken. Warm gently before serving or use cold.

What It's Good For

Most of us are used to eating salted cashew nuts, and do not realize how deliciously sweet these nuts are in their natural state. Raw cashews are low in oil and rich in potassium and magnesium, iron and zinc. Always rinse and dry raw cashews before use, as they can develop a little mould, which may affect the flavour. The oils in coconut cream do not have a cholesterol-raising effect. They contain lauric acid, which combats the Epstein-Barr virus.

Blueberries in Yoghurt Layered with Soft Marzipan and Pear Slices

Ingredients for 4 servings

175 g/6 ounces fresh or frozen blueberries

1 ripe dessert pear (red-skinned if possible)

225 g/8 ounces plain soy or sheep's milk yoghurt

55 g/2 ounces ground almonds (almond flour)

55 g/2 ounces dried dates, chopped

4 tbsp red grape juice

Toasted chopped or flaked almonds

Instructions

Put the chopped dates in a small saucepan over a low heat with 6 tbsp water, cover and cook until soft. Remove from the heat and beat with a wooden spoon to a smooth paste. Stir in the ground almonds. The mixture should be the consistency of thick double cream (heavy cream). Add a little more water if necessary.

Put the blueberries in a covered saucepan over a low heat until the juices run. Remove from the heat and leave to cool. Slice the pear thinly and put it in a saucepan over a low heat with the red grape juice to poach gently for 3-4 minutes or until tender. Remove from the heat then remove the pear slices from the pan with a slotted spoon.

What It's Good For

This recipe provides protein from the yoghurt (whichever type is used), flavonoids from the blueberries, and vitamin E, calcium, magnesium and other minerals from the almonds. It is also rich in vitamin C.

Almonds are a good source of protein, calcium, magnesium, zinc and other trace elements.

Consumer Therapy Cookbook

Stir the yoghurt, pour it over the cooled blueberries, and fold in gently. Divide the pear slices between four individual glass serving dishes, then pour a layer of date and almond paste over them. Top with the yoghurt and blueberry mixture. Chill in the fridge for at least 1 hour and sprinkle generously with toasted chopped or flaked almonds just before serving.

Recipe by Carolyn Gibbs

Baked Apples Filled with a Soft Cherry Marzipan

Ingredients for 4 servings

4 large dessert apples, washed and cored

100 g/3.5 oz cherries, stoned

75 g/2½ ounces/½ cup ground almonds (almond flour)

2 tbsp toasted flaked almonds

Soy cream (optional) to taste

*Dried cherries and lueberries can be found in the baking departments of larger supermarkets. Look for brands without sugar and preservatives.

Instructions

Preheat the oven to 175°C/350°F/Gas mark 4. Put the stoned cherries in a shallow baking dish and roast them for 30 minutes. Transfer them to a bowl, blitz the cherries to a paste with a hand blender then mash in the ground almonds until well incorporated.

Using a sharp knife, score a circle around the 'waist' of each apple to allow it to expand on cooking, then place the apples in an oiled shallow oven-proof dish and stuff the marzipan into the centre of each apple. Place the dish in the centre of the oven and bake for 45 minutes or until tender. Remove from the oven, cut the apples vertically down the middle then turn them over and slice them thickly, trying not to dislodge the filling. Arrange overlapping apple slices on individual serving

What It's Good For

Do not consume marzipan or any nut-rich recipes if you suffer from herpes, since nuts are rich in arginine, which can cause flare-ups of the herpes virus. Almonds are rich in calcium and magnesium and are a good source of protein. Apple peel is very rich in cancer-preventing carotenes and flavonoids, as well as pectin. Pectin can help to treat constipation, and it binds to toxins in your intestines and helps your body eliminate them. Try to use organic apples, since pesticide collects in the skin.

plates and serve warm with a topping of soy cream and toasted flaked almonds.

Variation

Use blueberries or apricots instead of cherries. Spoon the filling into peach halves instead of apples. Brush the peaches with groundnut oil and bake in a very hot oven for 15 minutes.

Recipe by Linda Lazarides and Carolyn Gibbs

Sweet Mango Pudding with Almonds and Cardamom

Ingredients for 4 servings

300 ml/½ pint/1 cup soy or nut milk

45 g/1½ ounces/1 rounded tbsp brown rice flour

1 tbsp ground almonds (almond flour)

1 tsp ground cardamom

1 extra-large or two small mangoes

Soy cream (optional)

Flaked almonds, toasted

Instructions

Peel the mango, cut all the flesh off the stone and put it in a bowl. Using a blender or liquidizer, purée the mango flesh until smooth. (If it is not soft enough you can soften it by stewing in a pan for 20 minutes over a low heat with a tablespoon of water.)

Put the soy or nut milk in a saucepan over a medium heat, and whisk the brown rice flour, ground almonds and ground cardamom into it. Bring to the boil, stirring, then turn the heat down low and continue stirring for another 6 minutes to thicken.

Remove from the heat, then stir the mango purée into the contents of the saucepan. Beat well until smooth and uniform.

Pour the pudding into individual glass dishes. Pour a little soy cream on top and swirl it. Can also be served cold, garnished with toasted almonds and some finely diced dried fruit such as dates or unsulphured apricots.

What It's Good For

Like brown rice, brown rice flour is a good source of B vitamins and also methionine, a protein constituent (amino acid) which your liver needs to make an important antioxidant enzyme. Mangoes are a good source of vitamin C and carotenes—antioxidants related to the beta carotene in carrots. Cardamom has anti-microbial properties and is good for dysbiosis and candidiasis sufferers.

Melon Balls in Ginger and Orange Sauce

Ingredients for 2 servings

1 chilled cantaloupe melon large enough to serve 2 people

275 ml/½ pint/1 cup orange juice* (freshly squeezed if possible)

1 tbsp shredded orange zest

1 rounded tsp arrowroot powder

1 tsp finely grated fresh ginger

*If you can get ruby red oranges, this makes a lovely colour contrast with the melon.

Special equipment

A melon baller

Instructions

Put one tbsp of the orange juice into a small bowl with the arrowroot powder and the rest in a saucepan over a medium heat. Stir the arrowroot powder and juice together until smooth, then add to the saucepan along with the ginger and zest. Stir until the mixture just begins to simmer then immediately remove from the heat.

Allow the sauce to cool.

Using a melon baller, make as many balls as you can from the melon. Place in individual serving dishes and spoon the sauce over them.

What It's Good For

Orange zest is rich in flavonoid antioxidants (see page 226). Orange juice, especially if very fresh, is a good source of the B vitamin folic acid as well as vitamin C and carotenes antioxidants (related to beta carotene in carrots. Folic acid is often in short supply in diets which rely on convenience food, because it is very vulnerable to heat and light. Ginger is a great aid to the digestion and helps to stimulate the circulation.

Yoghurt Cheesecake with Black Forest Fruits

Makes one 8 inch diameter cake

For the base

80 g/3 ounces/fine oatmeal

55 g/2 ounces raisins

55 g/2 ounces coconut oil, chilled

25 g/1 ounce spelt flour

For the topping

225 g/8 ounces frozen 'Black Forest' fruits

450 g/1 pound/2 cups sheep's yoghurt

15 g/½ ounce gelatine powder

1 tsp natural vanilla extract

Red grape juice as required

*e.g. a mixture of blueberries, black cherries, blackberries, black grapes, strawberries, blackcurrants. This type of mixture is sold under different names in supermarkets. You could also use the equivalent in fresh fruit.

Special equipment

A food processor

Instructions

Preheat the oven to gas mark 5. Put the oatmeal, spelt flour and raisins in a food processor with the S blade, and process until the raisins are finely chopped and blended with the flours. Transfer to a bowl, add the vanilla extract and solid coconut oil and mash into the flour with a fork until the mixture resembles fine breadcrumbs. Press it evenly on to the base of an oiled 20 cm/8 inch diameter foil pie dish or sandwich tin (not one with a removable bottom). Bake for 10-15 minutes until golden then allow to cool.

Pour the yoghurt into a sieve lined with kitchen paper suspended over a bowl and leave it to drip for at least one hour.

Put the fruits in a covered saucepan over a low heat to cook gently in their own steam. Once they have released their juices, purée them in the pan with a hand blender. Bring the purée to the boil, then remove from the heat and sprinkle in the gelatine. Whisk briskly until it dissolves.

Combine strained yoghurt and fruit purée in a measuring jug. If the contents do not reach the 570 ml/1 pint/2 cups mark, top up with red grape juice. Whizz again with the blender until smooth, then pour into the sandwich tin over the pastry base and refrigerate until set.

You could make a gluten-free version using crushed roasted nuts and gluten-free biscuits (cookies) instead of a pastry base.

Chocolate Mousse

Ingredients for 3 servings

1 large avocado, peeled and cut into pieces

Half a can of coconut milk (or 1 small 160 ml can)

3 soft eating dates (e.g. Medjool), chopped, stones removed

2 tbsp organic cocoa powder

1 tbsp sunflower or walnut oil

Grated bitter chocolate to decorate

Special equipment

A food processor

Instructions

Warm the can of coconut milk in a bowl of hot water for a few minutes, then pour into a food processor bowl. Stir in the chopped dates and leave for 30 minutes for the dates to absorb some of the moisture.

Add the avocado pieces and oil, and whizz together (using the S blade). Stir in the cocoa powder and whizz again, using the pulse button to start with. You will need to scrap the sides down from time to time until all the ingredients are thoroughly incorporated and the mixture is smooth.

Spoon into individual dishes and leave for at least half an hour before serving, as this helps the flavours to mingle together.

Serve decorated with a little grated bitter chocolate.

This mousse freezes well. I freeze it in individual ramekins covered with clingfilm.

Variations

For fruity mousses, use silken tofu instead of avocado, and all-fruit jam or spread (such as apricot) instead of dates and cocoa.

What It's Good For

Chocaholics will love this recipe, and few will realize that it is made with health-giving avocado instead of the fats which can make overindulgence in ordinary chocolate so harmful. Cocoa powder is rich in iron, magnesium and antioxidant flavonoids. But do not use it if you suffer from migraine or breast lumps, cysts or tenderness. Cocoa and chocolate contain caffeine-like compounds which in some people seem to encourage these problems.

Banana, Peanut Butter and Goji Berry Ice Cream

Ingredients for 4-6 scoops

2 bananas

Half a can coconut milk (or 1 small 160 ml can)

1 tbsp goji berries

1 tbsp smooth peanut butter

2 tbsp sunflower or walnut oil

Special equipment

A food processor

Instructions

Peel the bananas, cut into chunks and freeze.

Warm the can of coconut milk in a bowl of hot water for a few minutes, then pour into a food processor bowl. Stir in the goji berries and leave to soak in the coconut milk for at least an hour to help plump them up a little.

Using a fork, incorporate the oil into the peanut butter until you have a smooth mixture.

Add the frozen banana pieces into the food processor then the peanut butter/oil mixture. Blend with the S blade until smooth, scraping down the sides from time to time.

This produces a soft ice cream which is best served immediately. You could keep it in the freezer for a short while but it becomes solid and unmanageable if frozen for too long. If you do need to freeze it, spread it into a shallow tray and allow it to soften for half an hour before serving.

What It's Good For

Bananas are a natural and delicious sweetener. Goji Berries are used by the people of Tibet to increase longevity and as a general health tonic. They hold annual celebrations in goji's honour. Coconut milk adds richness to food, similar to dairy cream, but the body does not handle it as fat and it does not raise LDL (bad) cholesterol.

Little extras

Recipes for pastry, mayonnaise, ketchup, flatbread, apple sauce, and other useful extras.

If you really miss cheese, I hope you will enjoy the tasty cheese substitute (Melting Red Leicester) on page 209. You can use it as a topping on hot food, or eat it with rice crackers and pumpernickel.

Home-Made Tomato Ketchup

Makes 225 ml/8 fluid oz/ ¾ cup

1 small can of tomato purée (paste) (140 g/5 ounces)

3 tbsp cider vinegar or wine vinegar

3 tbsp water

½ tsp gluten-free mustard powder

Freshly ground nutmeg

Low-sodium salt

Freshly ground black pepper

Instructions

Mix the ingredients thoroughly and store in a jar in the fridge for up to four days.

Variations

Spice the ketchup up with cayenne pepper or some chopped gherkins or capers.

What It's Good For

No artificial preservatives, colourings or flavourings, no sugar or salt, this is quick to make but more delicious than any commercial brand. Tomato purée is very rich in a carotene known as lycopene, which is especially powerful in preventing prostate and breast cancer and is thought to be an even stronger neutralizer of free radicals than beta carotene.

Sour Cream

Ingredients for 6 servings

250 g/9 ounces silken tofu*

2 tbsp apple juice

Up to 6 tbsp water

4 tbsp cold-pressed unrefined sunflower oil

2 tbsp fresh lemon juice

½ tsp natural vanilla extract

*Silken tofu has a creamy blancmange-like texture. It comes in soft, medium and firm varieties. The firmer the tofu, the more water you will need to blend into it for this recipe.

Instructions

Whizz all the ingredients except the water in a blender. If it is too thick, whizz in the water little by little until you reach the desired consistency. For savoury recipes you might also want to add a pinch of low-sodium salt.

Variations

Garlic Sour Cream

Add half a clove of chopped raw garlic and a pinch of low sodium salt to the other ingredients in the blender before whizzing.

Mustard Sour Cream

Add a teaspoon of mustard powder to the other ingredients in the blender before whizzing.

What It's Good For

It is not widely known that the taste of cow's milk comes from a combination of lactose (milk sugar) and coumarin, a flavonoid-like substance found in hay and clover. Coumarin has a flavour almost identical to vanilla, which is why a little vanilla extract is used in this recipe.

See page 40 for the benefits of consuming soy products.

Garlic Crème

Makes 300 ml/½ pint/1 cup garlic crème

50 g/1¾ ounces/½ cup soy flour

275 ml/½ pint/1 cup boiling water

100 ml/3 fluid oz/a cup cold-pressed unrefined sunflower oil

1 tbsp flax seed oil (optional)

1 tbsp lemon juice

1 clove fresh garlic, roughly chopped

½ tsp low-sodium salt

Instructions

The flavours of soy and garlic complement each other perfectly in this delicious recipe, which is one of the best medicinal foods in this book.

Add the soy flour to the boiling water in a saucepan, and whisk to ensure no lumps remain. Simmer gently for 20 minutes, stirring from time to time and ensure it does not boil over. Remove from the heat and allow to cool.

Transfer to the goblet of a liquidizer and whizz with the lemon juice, salt, garlic and half the sunflower oil. When smooth add the rest of the sunflower oil plus the flax seed oil (if you are using it) and whizz again for 1-2 minutes. This Garlic Crème will keep for a few days in the fridge, and you can also stir in other flavourings such as chopped herbs or mustard. Stir before use. Use cold as a topping or a dressing or as a sauce with fish.

What It's Good For

Raw garlic contains allicin, destroyed by cooking but with many health benefits. After consumption, it travels to all parts of your body, helping to sterilize them. Raw garlic has been used to treat bronchitis, dysentery, typhoid, cholera, food poisoning and worms, as well as cryptosporidial diarrhoea associated with AIDS. It can help to heal the bowels after amoebic dysentery and to combat the thrush-causing yeast *Candida albicans*. Flax seed oil is one of the few good sources of omega 3 essential polyunsaturated oils.

Apple Sauce and Apple Butter

Makes 570 ml/1 pint/2 cups apple sauce plus 275 ml/½ pint/1 cup of apple butter

2 kg/4½ pounds sweet apples with a good flavour, such as Cox's

150 ml/¼ pint/½ cup water

Special Equipment

A pressure cooker

Instructions

Core and segment the apples (this task is very quick if you use a coring/segmenting gadget) but do not peel them. Put the segments in a pressure cooker with the water, bring up to full steam and cook for 10 minutes.

Cool the pressure cooker and remove the lid. Put the contents in a food processor with the S blade and whizz until smooth. You will probably need to do this in two batches. It takes a few minutes to really pulverize the peel.

Return the apple purée to the pan, and leave over a medium heat for one hour, stirring from time to time. Turn the heat down to prevent violent sputtering. At the end of this time, use a ladle to spoon out 570 ml/1 pint/2 cups of the purée, which you can now use as apple sauce. To make apple butter, leave the rest to continue reducing over the heat for another 2-3 hours. At the end of this time you should have a very thick mixture which stiffens on cooling and becomes spreadable like butter.

What It's Good For

Apple peel is rich in the cancer-preventing flavonoid quercetin, as well as the soluble fibre pectin. Pectin is used to set jam, and is the reason why this apple sauce recipe can thicken soy or nut milk and turn it into custard (see page 186). Pectin can also bind to toxins in your intestines and help you eliminate them. The skin is the most nutritious part of the apple, but may harbour pesticides, so make this recipe with organic apples if you can.

Basic Tomato Sauce

Ingredients for 2 servings

2 x 400 g/14 ounce cans of chopped Italian plum tomatoes

3 cloves garlic, finely chopped

A few pieces dried porcini mushrooms, chopped small

1 tbsp capers, chopped

1 tbsp coriander (cilantro) chopped

2 tbsp extra virgin olive oil

Low-sodium salt

Freshly ground black pepper

Instructions

Put all the ingredients except the black pepper into a saucepan, bring to the boil, then simmer with the lid off until reduced to a thick, glossy consistency. Stir in freshly-ground black pepper. This sauce can be served with gluten-free pasta, rösti recipes or grilled fish.

You can make this with fresh tomatoes too. Cut them into pieces and place in a saucepan with a few tablespoons of water. Put the lid on and leave over a low heat until the tomatoes have softened and released their juice. Pass them through a sieve, replace in the pan then add the other ingredients and proceed to reduce as previously described.

What It's Good For

Tomato sauce is very rich in a carotene known as lycopene, which is especially powerful in preventing prostate and breast cancer and is thought to be an even stronger neutralizer of free radicals than beta carotene.

This concentrated sauce is also an excellent source of potassium, vitamin C and minerals.

Melting Red Leicester

Ingredients to make 450 g/ 1 lb

280 ml/½ pint/1 cup water

2 tbsp agar flakes

Half a sweet red (bell) pepper

115 g/4 ounces/½ cup raw cashew nuts which have been soaked overnight and drained

2 tbsp gluten-free miso (get a pale variety if you can)

1 tbsp fresh lemon juice

1 tsp onion granules

1 tsp garlic granules

1 level tsp low-sodium salt

½ tsp gluten-free mustard powder

Special equipment

A lightly oiled container to use as a mould (mold)

Instructions

Put the water in a small saucepan over a medium heat, sprinkle in the agar flakes without stirring, and bring to a gentle simmer.

Keep simmering for five minutes, stirring until all the agar has dissolved.

Put the mixture in a liquidizer or food processor together with the remaining ingredients, and process until smooth. This usually takes about five minutes. Keep scraping down the sides to ensure even processing.

Pour immediately into the mould and allow to cool. Cover and chill overnight. Can be served on rice crackers or with corn chips or mini-poppadoms. It will also melt on hot dishes like baked potatoes or wheat-free pasta.

You will probably need to search online to find a source of pale miso, but if you can't find it, use regular gluten-free miso.

What It's Good For

With a pleasantly cheesy flavour, this Red Leicester is low in fat and melts in the mouth with a light, pudding-like texture. The main ingredients are carotene-rich sweet red pepper (capsicum) and protein-rich cashew nuts providing potassium, magnesium, iron and zinc.

Agar is a natural gelling agent made from seaweed.

Mayonnaise

Makes about 300 ml/½ pint/1 cup

100 g/3½ ounces silken tofu*

1 tbsp fresh lemon juice

100 ml/3½ fluid oz mild-flavoured extra virgin olive oil

Up to 100 ml/3½ fluid oz water

Low-sodium salt

*If you are using a soft silken tofu, you will need only a fraction of the water. If you are using an extra-firm silken tofu such as Sanchi Organic Tofu, you will need all of it.

Instructions

Using a blender, liquidize the tofu with the lemon juice, some or all of the water (depending on the softness of the tofu) and the low-sodium salt, then whizz in the olive oil.

This makes a thick basic mayonnaise. It can easily be thinned by whizzing in more water, or stretched by whizzing in more oil.

Variations

Mayonnaise can be flavoured with a teaspoon of pale miso (see page 244) or with fresh garlic, dried garlic or onion granules, mustard, horseradish or fresh spring onion (scallion) among others.

Add tarragon to make a Béarnaise type sauce, or add chopped capers to make a tartar sauce.

What It's Good For

Tofu (made from soy) is a rich source of sex hormone-balancing flavonoids known as isoflavones. So a diet rich in tofu can help to prevent all kinds of problems, from menopausal hot flushes, to breast cancer and prostate cancer.

Extra virgin olive oil is an important part of the Mediterranean diet, which helps prevent health problems in old age and is also now known to help prevent a deterioration of mental faculties.

Short Crust Pastry (pie-crust)

When rolled out makes 2 pastry rounds with a diameter of about 25 cm/10 inches.

100 g/3½ ounces/scant 1 cup
brown rice flour

100 g/3½ ounces/scant 1 cup
spelt flour

100 g/3½ ounces/scant 1 cup
pieces of solid coconut oil*
pieces at room
temperature

120 ml/4 fluid ounces/scant ½
cup water

Special equipment

A food processor

*Use refined (not virgin) coconut oil to avoid imparting a coconut flavour to this pastry.

Instructions

Preheat the oven to 190°C/375°F gas mark 5.

Sift the dry ingredients then add them to the food processor with the coconut oil pieces. Whizz until the mixture resembles fine breadcrumbs. Transfer to a bowl and add the water little by little, working it into the mixture with a fork until you can form a large, soft ball of dough with your hands. (You may not need all the water, or you may need a little extra.)

Knead briefly then refrigerate for at least half an hour before rolling out.

Use this pastry as you would any other shortcrust pastry: to make pasties, pies, pastry cases for tarts, and so on. Bake for 20-25 minutes or until golden.

After cooking this pastry becomes quite hard when refrigerated, so it is best brought to room temperature before you try to cut it.

What It's Good For

This makes a very respectable shortcrust pastry with a good, light texture. Coconut oil is much healthier than margarine. Although solid at room temperature it is not a saturated fat, and does not cause increases in blood cholesterol levels. It can actually aid weight loss as the body does not treat it like other fats.

Gluten Free Pastry (pie-crust)

When rolled out each 100 grams (3.5 ounces) of combined flours makes 1 pastry round with a diameter of about 25 cm/10 inches.

Equal weights of brown rice flour, buckwheat flour and gram (chickpea) or soy flour

Coconut oil pieces* totalling exactly half the weight of the combined flours

Water

Special equipment

A food processor

*Use refined (not virgin) coconut oil to avoid imparting a coconut flavour to this pastry.

Instructions

Preheat the oven to 190°C/375°F gas mark 5.

Sift the dry ingredients then add them to the food processor with the coconut oil pieces. Whizz until the mixture resembles fine breadcrumbs. Transfer to a bowl and add the water little by little, working it into the mixture with a fork until you can form a large, soft, pliable ball of dough with your hands.

This dough benefits from squeezing and kneading and is best not chilled before rolling out. But it is much more fragile than regular pastry dough, so don't roll it out too thin or it will break when you try to lift it or line a tin with it. Be prepared to do a little pressing and patching.

Use this pastry as you would any other shortcrust pastry: to make pasties, pies, pastry cases for tarts, and so on. It will provide a good short texture when cooked. Bake for 20-25 minutes or until golden.

What It's Good For

It is common for people with a wheat intolerance to also have a gluten intolerance even if they are not coeliac (celiac). A gluten intolerance only causes bowel problems in severe cases. Before reaching that stage you may just suffer from bloating, headaches, excessive sleeping, fatigue or sluggishness, and never realize that these are being caused by consuming gluten.

It is well worth going on a two-week gluten-free diet to see if you feel different. So-called 'detox diets' are usually gluten-free, and this may be why some people feel very good when they follow them.

More about gluten-free pastry

A number of commercial gluten-free flours are available, both plain, self-raising and bread type flours. In the UK, the Dove's Farm brand is commonly found in supermarkets. In the US, Bob's Red Mill is a well-known brand.

Commercial gluten-free flour blends are made from a combination of flour and starch, typically two thirds brown rice, buckwheat, and maize meal, and one third cornflour (corn starch), tapioca and potato starch. You can make your own combination, for instance using two thirds brown rice flour and one third corn starch.

When making pastry or English biscuits you may run into problems using these blends. Add too little water and the dough cannot be rolled out. Add too much and the baked product will be very tough. The manufacturers usually suggest getting round this problem by adding an egg when making pastry.

Instead of an egg you can replace 20-25 per cent of the commercial blend with gram (chickpea) or soy flour. Add enough water to make the dough manageable, but do not roll it out too thin or it will break.

Xanthan gum

Many brands of commercial gluten-free flour have added xanthan gum. This helps to replace gluten in cakes and bread making, and to retain moisture. But for pastry you want a crumbly texture. The very reason for not over-working the dough when making wheat flour pastry is that this will spoil the texture of the finished product. So there is no need to add xantham gum when making pastry.

Sweet Chestnut Crust

When rolled out makes 2 pastry rounds with a diameter of about 25 cm/10 inches.

100 g/3½ ounces/scant 1 cup chestnut flour[*]

100 g/3½ ounces/scant 1 cup spelt flour

100 g/3½ ounces/scant 1 cup solid coconut oil,[**] at room temperature

120 ml/4 fluid ounces/scant ½ cup white grape juice

20 g/¾ ounce soy or nut milk powder

½ tsp baking powder

[*]Available from health food stores or online

[**]Use refined (not virgin) coconut oil to avoid imparting a coconut flavour

Instructions

Preheat the oven to 190°C/375°F gas mark 5.

Sift the dry ingredients into a bowl, then add them with the coconut oil to a food processor and whizz until the mixture resembles fine breadcrumbs. Add the grape juice little by little, working it into the mixture with a rubber spatula until you can form a large, soft ball of dough with your hands. Knead briefly then refrigerate for at least half an hour.

Oil the tin (metal produces the best results) which will be in contact with the pastry while cooking. Remove the dough from the fridge, and knead until you can roll the pastry out without it breaking up.

Roll out the pastry evenly, using extra spelt flour to prevent it sticking (it may be easier to roll it out between two sheets of clingfilm). Use to make cases for sweet desserts, tarts and tartlets. Bake for about 25 minutes or until golden.

What It's Good For

The main benefits of this recipe come from the chestnut flour, rich in potassium, magnesium and iron, and spelt flour, rich in B vitamins and vitamin E.

Coconut oil does not raise cholesterol levels like butter and other animal fats. It contains beneficial plant sterols, which help to prevent cholesterol rises. It also contains lauric acid, which combats the Epstein-Barr virus.

Pan-Baked Pea Bread

Ingredients for 8 thin rounds about 8 cm/4 inches wide

200g/7 ounces/1 cup chickpea (gram) flour

100 ml/3½ fluid oz/scant ½ cup water

2 tbsp arrowroot powder

1 tbsp groundnut oil

Gluten-free flour for rolling out

Low-sodium salt

Instructions

Mix the dry ingredients then add the water and oil, and mix thoroughly, using the back of a spoon to work the ingredients together into a thick, stiff and sticky dough.

Divide the dough into 8 portions. Using gluten-free flour to prevent sticking, roll the mixture into balls and flatten with your hand. Then, using a rolling pin, roll into thin rounds.

Preheat a dry griddle pan or good quality frying pan over a medium heat until very hot. Put a dough round in the pan and cook for about one minute or until it puffs up and small brown spots appear on the bottom. Turn and cook the other side. These light and tasty breads are delicious served warm with soup, and can also be folded over and stuffed with salad ingredients plus any of the following:

- Grated hard goat's cheese
- One of the Speciality Patés (page 84)
- Guacamole (page 92),
- Hummus (page 79).

What It's Good For

Gram (chick pea) flour is very rich in protein. It is also a good source of many other nutrients, including calcium, magnesium, iron, copper and some of the B vitamins.

Flatbreads

Ingredients for approx 9 x 6-inch wide rounds of bread

10 oz/275 g wholemeal spelt flour

2 tbsp thick soy or sheep's milk yoghurt

100 ml/3½ fluid oz/scant ½ cup water

Recipe by Carolyn Gibbs

Instructions

Add the yoghurt and water to the flour and mix to a soft, pliable dough. Turn out on to a well-floured board and knead for about 8 minutes until the dough is smooth and elastic, using more flour if necessary to prevent sticking. Put in a bowl covered with a damp cloth for 30 minutes.

Break off egg-sized pieces of dough, and roll into rounds measuring about 12 cm/6 inches in diameter and ½ cm/¼ inch thick. Pre-heat an unoiled griddle pan or good quality frying pan on a moderate heat for about 2 minutes. When the pan is hot, place a round of dough on it and cook for about a minute until the bread puffs up slightly. Briefly dab it all over very gently with a spatula to make it puff up more. Then immediately turn it over and repeat this on the other side.

Stack the rounds separated by absorbent kitchen paper. Keep warm until you are ready to serve them.

To Freeze

Slightly undercook the flatbreads. Allow to cool, place in polythene freezer bags and then in the freezer. To use, finish cooking the breads under a hot grill (broiler), but not too close to the heat as they will puff up.

What It's Good For

Spelt flour is sometimes known as 'ancient wheat', but often does not provoke symptoms in wheat intolerance sufferers. It has all the goodness of wholemeal flour: B vitamins, vitamin E and minerals, and of course bran fibre.

Cacik (yoghurt and cucumber sauce)

Ingredients for 4 servings

One standard tub of sheep's
  yoghurt (about 250 grams,
  or half a pint/1 cup in
  volume)

Half a cucumber, finely
  shredded or coarsely
  grated

1 clove garlic, crushed

2 tsp fresh mint, finely
  chopped, or 1 tsp dried
  mint

Low-sodium salt

Freshly ground black pepper

Instructions

Combine all the ingredients except the salt and mix well. Add the salt just before serving.

Use as a dip or as a sauce for Falafels (see page 94) or Spiced Bean Röstis (page 88). For a thicker Cacik, first strain the yoghurt by draining it for an hour in a sieve lined with kitchen paper.

What It's Good For

Sheep's yoghurt, while rich in protein like cow's milk yoghurt, is often safe to eat for people with a cow's milk intolerance. Yoghurt is also rich in beneficial bacteria for the intestines. Cucumber is rich in potassium and other minerals, and is a particularly good source of bone- and tissue-building silicon. But do not peel your cucumbers, as these nutrients are mostly concentrated in the skin. Mint is used by herbalists as a remedy to help the digestion and soothe inflammation in the intestines.

Vinaigrette Salad Dressing

Ingredients for 125 ml/4½ fluid oz/½ cup

6 tbsp extra virgin olive oil

2 tbsp cider vinegar or wine vinegar

1 tsp gluten-free mustard powder

Low-sodium salt

Freshly ground black pepper

Commercial mustard powder sometimes contains wheat flour. Mustard powder purchased from a health food store usually does not.

Instructions

Mix the mustard powder to a smooth paste with a little of the vinegar in a bowl, then, using a fork or small whisk, beat in a little oil followed by the rest of the oil and then the remaining ingredients.

This makes a basic vinaigrette. You can add any other ingredients you like, such as fresh or dried chopped herbs or gherkins, capers, raw garlic or finely sliced spring onion (scallion). Whisk the vinaigrette again just before serving.

If you are serving vinaigrette with a green salad, do not put it on the salad until the last minute.

What It's Good For

Extra virgin olive oil has been in the news recently since scientists found that it can help to prevent our brain processes from deteriorating as we get older. Sometimes anti-candida diets forbid vinegar because it contains yeasts and most Candida sufferers have a yeast allergy. However, those in vinegar (and miso) are natural yeasts, much less likely to cause allergic reactions than the commercial yeasts found in wine, beer, bread, pizza dough etc. If they do, use lemon or lime juice instead.

What should I drink?

Scientists estimate that most of us need to drink at least 2 litres of liquid a day—more in hot weather, if you are breast-feeding, or if you suffer from heavy periods, diarrhoea or tend to sweat heavily. You should drink this amount even if you don't feel thirsty. Thirst only begins once dehydration has started. Symptoms of dehydration include lethargy, nausea (including morning sickness of pregnancy), stomach discomfort, gastritis, heartburn, indigestion, constipation and inflammation. Chiropractors sometimes cure back pain and painful joints by asking people to drink water instead of tea and coffee.

Drinking more than 2.5 litres (4½ pints) of liquid a day halves your risk of getting bladder cancer.

The best drink of all is plain water. Drink it on its own, or use it to dilute fruit juice. Drinking a glass of cold water is an instant remedy any time your stomach feels unsettled. It really works against indigestion!

A mixture of sparkling water and fresh fruit juice is delicious, and much better for you than commercial sodas, which are often high in sodium and sugar or artificial chemicals. Weak fruit or herb teas such as rosehip, blackcurrant, fennel or chamomile—preferably without sugar—are also good choices, and can be drunk hot or cold (with ice). Certain fruit or vegetable juices and herbal or spice teas can help combat health problems. You can find more about the properties of spices in the chapter on superfoods.

The worst drinks for your health are tea, coffee and alcohol, because of their diuretic effect. A diuretic stimulates your body to excrete fluid more rapidly, even when its fluid levels are already low.

Alcohol can particularly dehydrate you as it reduces the effectiveness of anti-diuretic hormone (ADH), a hormone which is meant to slow down your excretion of fluid when you are beginning to get dehydrated. Drinking a pint of water before going to bed after you have consumed a lot of alcohol can help to reduce the dehydration—and the resulting hangover.

Green tea and cinnamon tea

These are particularly beneficial. Green tea is known for its antioxidant and cancer-preventive properties. Cinnamon tea is excellent for helping to potentiate insulin, and so aids blood sugar balance.

Therapeutic juices

If you have a juice extractor, you can make your own healthy fruit and vegetable juices. Many of these have valuable therapeutic uses.

Carrot juice

Carrots are cheap and easy to juice. The juice is sweet and contains the vitamin A precursor carotene, and an eye-protective nutrient known as lutein. A little carrot juice goes a long way and can be stirred into orange juice if you don't like the flavour.

Cabbage juice

This is definitely an acquired taste but can be disguised with other juices. Has similar beneficial effects to broccoli juice.

Celery juice

Helps to alkalinize your body. Very helpful against arthritis.

Lemon juice

(Include some of the pith and peel). Contains limonene, which is said to help dissolve gall-stones. Can be used to add flavour to other juices.

Broccoli juice

Helps to break down excess oestrogen and so to combat women's hormonal problems such as fibroids, breast cysts, endometriosis, breast cancer, PMS. Also contains lutein, which protects the eyes.

Radish juice

Stimulates bile production, combats harmful intestinal bacteria. Dries up congestion and helps eliminate cold symptoms. You only need a little—it is very powerful. You can use any type of radish, but the best is the mooli/daikon radish—a radish that looks like a big white carrot. It is sometimes known as a daikon radish.

Drinks recipes

Recipes for teas to help your digestion and prevent gas.

Nutrient-packed juices to combat arthritis and help your liver.

Alternatives to milk and commercial fizzy drinks.

Digestive Tea

Ingredients for 2 cup/ mugfuls

600 ml/1 pint/2 cups very hot water

1 tsp fresh ginger, grated (or ½ tsp ground ginger)

1 tsp fennel seeds

½ tsp ground cinnamon

¼ tsp ground cloves

Instructions

Using a mortar and pestle, crush the fennel seeds and mix with the other spices. Put the mixture in a small teapot and pour the boiling water over it. Stir thoroughly, cover and leave for 5 minutes, then strain through a very fine strainer and drink.

What It's Good For

These spices are prescribed by medical herbalists to soothe the digestion after a meal and to treat flatulence. If you are not used to eating the foods in this book and have trouble digesting them, this tea will be very helpful while your body is adapting. Sip it slowly during and after your meal. If you'd like it to be even more effective, you could also add a pinch of cayenne pepper, but watch out for the extra bite!

Home-Made Apple, Celery, Parsley and Radish Juice

Ingredients for 1 serving

1 large sweet apple, unpeeled and organically grown if possible

2 sticks celery

1 bunch parsley

5 cm/2 inch segment of mooli/daikon radish

Small piece of lemon, including peel*

*Optional - you may find that it helps the flavour

Instructions

Wash the ingredients, cut them into chunks and put them through a juice extractor. Stir and leave to stand for 20 minutes to break down the peppery taste of the radish before drinking.

Special Equipment

A juice extractor

What It's Good For

It would be hard to find a drink more rich in health-giving nutrients. This drink is: rich in vitamin C, helps to alkalinize your body, fights fluid retention (which causes pain and swellings in nerves, joints and breasts, as well as migraine and headaches), helps fight arthritis. If you have a cold the radish component will help to eliminate congestion. Radish juice also helps balance the thyroid gland.

Beetroot, Celery And Lemon Juice

Prepare quantities of ingredients according to how many people you are catering for

Bottled beetroot (beet) juice (or juice from raw beetroot made with a juice extractor)

Home-made celery juice

Fresh lemon juice

Instructions

Combine equal quantities of bottled beetroot juice and home-made celery juice made from fresh celery with a juice extractor, or use the proportions you prefer. Flavour with a little fresh lemon juice to taste.

If you juice your own raw beetroot, it will be very strong. Only a little is required, and should be diluted with water. It must be left to stand for 20 minutes before drinking or else it will have a very peppery taste.

Special Equipment

A juice extractor

What It's Good For

Beetroot juice is a powerful aid to your liver. Celery juice helps to alkalinize the body, thus combating the acidity that often leads to arthritis. It also contains coumarin, a substance which fights fluid retention by keeping your blood vessels strong and stimulating your lymphatic system. Fluid retention can simulate arthritis by pressing on joints and causing pain and swelling. Beetroot is one of the best plant sources of iron, needed for energy and for oxygen transport in your body.

Home-Made Broccoli Stem And Sharp Apple

Prepare quantities of ingredients according to how many people you are catering for

Equal quantities of

Broccoli stems

Sharp apples such as Granny
   Smiths

Instructions

Broccoli juice is very sweet, which is why it is good mixed with a fairly sharp apple juice. Simply cut the broccoli stems and apples into chunks and feed into your juice extractor in the proportions you prefer. You may need to experiment a little. If necessary, add a little lemon juice to disguise the broccoli flavour.

Special Equipment

A juice extractor

What It's Good For

Save your broccoli heads for eating and the thick stems for juicing, especially if
you have any female troubles linked to poor oestrogen metabolism, such as:
breast cysts or lumps, endometriosis, fibroids, family history of breast cancer.
Broccoli is a superb liver food and contains substances which help your liver to
break down excess oestradiol, the form of oestrogen which in excess can
encourage these problems.

Carrot And Orange Juice

Prepare quantities of ingredients according to how many people you are catering for

Carrots

Fresh oranges

Try to get organic oranges, or at least unwaxed ones. If you cannot obtain them, scrub ordinary oranges carefully in very hot water with detergent to remove the thin layer of pesticide-treated wax coating the skin, and then rinse.

Instructions

This is a lovely sweet combination. Juice your carrots in the juice-extractor together with some of the orange flesh and peel. Then juice the rest of the orange with a normal citrus juicer.

Mix together in the proportions you prefer and drink straight away.

If you do not have a juice extractor, use commercial juices and use your liquidizer to whizz in a piece of orange with the pith and peel still attached.

Special Equipment

A juice extractor

What It's Good For

Carrots are rich in beta carotene and other carotenes (a type of antioxidant) as well as in many minerals. Beta carotene can also be converted into vitamin A, although if you have an underactive thyroid this process may not be as efficient as it should be.

Fresh oranges are rich in the important B vitamin folic acid. The pith and peel is an excellent source of a type of antioxidant known as flavonoids, which can fight fluid retention.

Flavonoid-Rich Orange Juice

Ingredients

Ready-made orange juice,
   plus

Fresh oranges

Try to get organic oranges, or
at least unwaxed ones. If you
cannot obtain them, scrub
ordinary oranges carefully in
very hot water with detergent
to remove the thin layer of
pesticide-treated wax coating
the skin, and then rinse.

Instructions

Liquidize a piece of fresh orange with pith and peel into a glass of normal orange juice. This will contain a far larger quantity of flavonoids than you could get in a flavonoid supplement pill!

What It's Good For

Fresh orange juice is rich in folic acid, one of the nutrients most likely to be in short supply in our diet. It is now known that one of the biggest causes of the high blood cholesterol levels that lead to heart attacks is a folic acid deficiency, which can be detected by measuring levels of a substance known as homocysteine in your blood. People with high homocysteine levels are at the highest risk of heart attacks. Levels can often be brought down by consuming more folic acid and vitamins B_6 and B_{12}.

Home-Made Ginger Tea With Lemon Zest

Ingredients to make one cup or mugful

One tsp fresh grated ginger

One tsp fresh, finely shredded lemon zest*

*Try to get organic lemons, or at least unwaxed ones. If you cannot obtain them, scrub ordinary lemons carefully in very hot water with detergent to remove the thin layer of pesticide-treated wax coating the skin, and then rinse.

Instructions

Pour a cupful of boiling water on to a teaspoon of grated fresh ginger and a teaspoon of fresh lemon zest shreds. Leave to infuse for five minutes, then strain and drink.

What It's Good For

Ginger is known as a 'hot bitter' herb, which helps your stomach to produce digestive juices and so aids digestion. Much research has been carried out into its benefits, especially against rheumatoid arthritis and travel sickness. In Chinese medicine, ginger is considered to warm and stimulate the circulation and to remove catarrh and combat bronchitis. Lemon zest is rich in flavonoids— anti-cancer antioxidants which also help the circulation by keeping blood vessels walls strong.

Nut Milk

Ingredients for 2 servings

570 ml/1 pint/2 cups water

55 g/2 ounces/scant ½ cup chopped almonds*

*Can be made by whizzing blanched almonds in a food processor

Instructions

Soak the chopped almonds in the water overnight in the goblet of your liquidizer.

In the morning whizz them together until the almonds have turned into a fine pulp, and strain the milk through a fine sieve.

This delicious milk is naturally sweet and excellent for drinking. The pulp can be added to rice pudding.

Try the same method with other nuts or seeds, such as brazils, cashews and sunflower seeds. You could also use oatmeal to make oat milk.

Brazil nuts do not need soaking but do rinse and dry them before use, to improve the flavour.

What It's Good For

While not as rich in protein as cow's milk, soy milk and nut milks do contain a good range of nutrients, especially calcium and magnesium, essential polyunsaturated oils, zinc and vitamin E. But if you have a young baby these alternative milks are not a suitable substitute for formula milks. Although almonds are calorie-rich (about 600 Calories per 100 grams) feeding nut milk too early, before the baby's digestion has matured, could result in developing an allergy.

Soda Pop

Ingredients

Equal quantities of sparkling mineral water and any combination of:

Red or white grape juice

Apple juice

Orange juice

Mango, passion fruit, peach, pineapple or raspberry juices

Use either ready-made juices or make your own with a juice extractor

Instructions

Just mix your favourite combinations together and drink immediately. Try for some interesting colours such as mixing raspberry and orange juice.

You could also liquidize small amounts of soft fruit into the juice before mixing it with the mineral water.

What It's Good For

These drinks are especially good for hyperactive children, who often react badly to the colourings and sugar in canned fizzy drinks. Commercial drinks can also contain large amounts of phosphorus. Although we all need phosphorus, if it gets out of balance with the other minerals in your body it can make calcium leach from your bones, encouraging bone softness and osteoporosis (brittle bone disease). Fresh fruit juices are of course rich in vitamin C and in flavonoid and carotene antioxidants.

Appendices

Appendix I: The Vitamins and Minerals

Name	Key Words	Good Sources	Therapeutic Uses (according to research)
Vitamin A (Retinol)	Eyesight, growth, immune system, mucous membranes, normal development of tissues, protein synthesis	Butter, cheese, fish liver oils, liver, protein margarine. Beta carotene in green and yellow vegetables can be converted to vitamin A in the body.	Helps acne, psoriasis, gastric ulcers. Helps prevent the common cold. Reduces complications from measles. Improves eyesight.
Vitamin B₁ (Thiamine)	Conversion of carbohydrate to energy. Energy production. Brain, heart, muscle and nerve function. Release of acetylcholine from nerve cells. Inhibits oxidation of dopamine.	Beans, brown rice, lentils, pork, whole grains	Has been used as a painkiller for headaches and joint pain. Helps improve nerve function in epilepsy. Helps trigeminal neuralgia. Helps optic neuritis. Reduces nerve damage in diabetics.
Vitamin B₂ (Riboflavin)	Growth. Metabolism of fats, protein and carbohydrate. Activates vitamin B₆. Conversion of carbohydrate to energy and tryptophan to vitamin B₃.	Dairy products, eggs, liver, meat, soybean flour, whole grains	May help acne rosacea, carpal tunnel syndrome, cataracts, mitochondria, some types of anaemia.
Vitamin B₃ (Niacin)	Conversion of carbohydrate to energy. DNA synthesis. Health of skin, nerves, brain and digestive system. Synthesis of fatty acids and steroids.	Beef liver, chicken, meat, nuts, peanuts, salmon and other oily fish, sunflower seeds, whole grains	May act as a mild anti-histamine. May help relieve tinnitis, reduce cholesterol, reduce insulin requirements in some diabetics, reduce period (menstrual) pains, reduce schizophrenia (in megadoses), wheezing in asthmatics.
Vitamin B₅ (Pantothenic acid)	Conversion of carbohydrate to energy. Growth and development. Health of nervous system. Production of anti-stress hormones.	Eggs, liver, meat, nuts, whole grains, yeast	May alleviate allergic reactions and help stress, rheumatoid arthritis, anaemia.
Vitamin B₆ (Pyridoxine)	Metabolism of protein, carbohydrate, fat, calcium, magnesium, selenium, homocysteine, histamine, energy. Blood and haemoglobin formation. Conversion of glycogen to glucose, and tryptophan to	Avocados, bananas, fish, meat, nuts, seeds, whole grains	May help childhood autism, asthma, carpal tunnel syndrome, morning sickness of pregnancy, Parkinson's disease, premenstrual acne, premenstrual syndrome, insulin resistance, fluid retention, Tourette syndrome, anaemia (including sickle .

	Functions	Best food sources	May help / benefits
	vitamin B₃ or serotonin. Selenium transportation. Synthesis of prostaglandins from essential fatty acids. Zinc absorption		cell anaemia). May reduce sensitivity to monosodium glutamate
Vitamin B₁₂ (Cobalamin)	Detoxification of cyanide (found in tobacco smoke and in some foods). DNA synthesis. Growth and development. Healthy nerve cells.	Cheese, eggs, fish, liver, meat, Found only in animal foods, although some vegan products are fortified with extra B₁₂ by the manufacturers.	May help chronic pain, fatigue, mental confusion, multiple sclerosis, numbness of the extremities, some cases of mental illness, some cases of tinnitus.
Biotin	Metabolism of carbohydrate, protein, fat, energy. Formation of prostaglandins from essential fatty acids and glucose from amino acids, lactate and glycerol. Growth. Health of skin, hair, nerves, sweat glands, sex glands, bone marrow.	Widely distributed in meats, dairy produce and whole grains. Liver and egg yolk are particularly rich sources Egg white inhibits absorption of biotin.	May help some cases of hair loss and scalp disease seborrhoeic dermatitis and other skin complaints, diabetic nerve damage. May reduce blood sugar in some diabetics.
Folic acid (Folate)	Blood formation. Protein, RNA and DNA, glycine and methionine synthesis. Needed for conversion of tyrosine and tryptophan to adrenal hormones and serotonin.	Leafy green vegetables, especially raw spinach. Liver, freshly squeezed orange juice, soy flour, lentils, whole grains, yeast extract.	Prevents spina bifida in the unborn. Treats anaemia if folic acid is deficient Reduces homocysteine. May help reverse precancerous conditions of the cervix, depression and schizophrenia.
Vitamin C (Ascorbate)	Aids absorption of iron from vegetables. Antioxidant. Collagen formation. Immune system. Tyrosine and stress hormone production. Wound healing.	Broccoli, brussels sprouts, cabbage, fresh fruit (especially citrus), fresh (bell) peppers, kiwi fruit, raw leafy vegetables, tomatoes	Anti-histamine effect. Can control and cure the common cold. May help cancer and idiopathic thrombocytopenic purpura (blood disease), asthma, blood sugar control in diabetics, manic depression (bipolar disorder), Parkinson's disease (with vitamin E), wound healing, clearance of toxic chemicals. Enhances number, size and motility of white blood cells. Inhibits adrenochrome formation in schizophrenia. Lowers blood cholesterol. Protects eye lens against oxidative damage. Reverses pre-cancerous conditions.
Vitamin D (Calciferol)	Absorption of magnesium and other minerals. Bone health, calcium and kidney metabolism, liver oil, anti-cancer action. Immune function. Ant	Butter, liver, cod liver oil, halibut liver oil, herrings, kippers, mackerel, salmon, sardines tuna	Anti-inflammatory, anti-infection, anti-cancer. Supports heart and muscle health, hormone function, bone health.

	Functions	Can help	Sources
Vitamin E (Tocopherol)	Antioxidant, especially combating peroxidation of unsaturated fats in cell membranes. Development and maintenance of nerve and muscle function. Fertility, immunity, prostaglandin control, red cell membrane stability, reduces oxygen needs of muscles, spares vitamin A.	Can help Parkinson's disease, epilepsy, muscular dystrophy (with selenium), macular degeneration, osteoarthritis, neuropathy, premenstrual syndrome, cystic breast disease, hearing loss (with vitamin A), hepatitis, precancerous breast conditions, menopausal symptoms, systemic lupus erythematosus, sickle cell anaemia, complications of diabetes (and enhances insulin action). Reduces liver damage from carbon tetrachloride, pain from shingles and other chronic pain. Reduces scars when applied to skin, harmful effects of inhaling ozone, nitrogen oxide, and other constituents of smog or cigarette smoke. Enhances immune system. Increases HDL ('good') cholesterol. Inhibits platelet adhesiveness (blood 'stickiness'). Halves risk of heart attack in those with heart disease. Heals sunburn when applied to the skin. Helps reduce side effects of anti-schizophrenic drugs. Prevents cataracts.	Almonds, butter, leafy green vegetables, oats, peanuts, soybean oil, sunflower oil and wheatgerm and wheatgerm oil of whole grains
Vitamin K (phylloquinone or mena-quinone)	Production of four proteins involved in blood clotting. Bone calcification and mineralization.	Can accelerate healing of bone fractures, increase bone formation in post-menopausal osteoporotic woman, reduce calcium losses in urine.	Alfalfa, broccoli, brussels sprouts, cabbage, leafy green vegetables, cauliflower, green tea, liver, meats, soybean, rapeseed and olive oils, tomatoes, whole grains
Calcium	Acetylcholine synthesis, action of many hormones, activation of saliva and many enzymes, blood clotting, blood pressure regulation, conversion of glycogen to glucose, muscle contractions, nerve impulses, structure of cells, bones and teeth, vitamin B12 absorption	Can help muscle cramps, oestoporosis, high blood pressure, allergic symptoms, period (menstrual) pains, premenstrual emotional pains and fluid retention, migraine and hearing loss (with vitamin D), clearance of lead, mercury, aluminium and cadmium.	Broccoli, cheese (especially hard and many cheeses), canned fish (if bones are consumed), cow's milk, leafy green vegetables (legumes), nuts, pulses (legumes), root vegetables, yoghurt, sunflower and sesame seeds
Chromium	Promotes good blood sugar balance and enhances the effectiveness of insulin	Can increase the density of insulin receptors (thus aiding the function of insulin). Helps reduce high blood cholesterol, hypoglycaemia, hyperinsulinaemia, especially when given with magnesium.	Liver, mushrooms, whole grains, yeast

Copper	Assists iron absorption and transport. Avocados, liver molasses, nuts, Helps anaemia, rheumatism, rheumatoid arthritis. Maintenance of connective tissues, blood vessels olives, pulses (legumes), shellfish, and myelin sheath around nerve fibres. whole grains Cholesterol regulation. Production of energy, haemoglobinadrenal hormones, pigments in skin and hair, ceruloplasmin and detoxifying enzymes SOD and cytochrome oxidase. Histamine inactivation.
Iodine	Thyroid hormone production. Iodine is also Dairy products, fish and seafood, Can treat goitre. Can improve fibrocystic breast disease (certain actively concentrated from the blood by the pineapple, raisins, seaweed (e.g. specific forms of iodine only). stomach mucosa, salivary glands, choroid plexus kelp). Very large amounts of iodine of the brain and the lactating mammary glands, are found in the artificial food suggesting further functions as yet unknown. additive erythrosine (E127), used as a red colouring for cocktail and glacé cherries. A high consumption of these foods is not advised if they contain this additive.
Iron	Needed for cell proliferation, function of white Back sausage, cocoa powder and Can improve detoxification ability in some individuals, and some blood cells, liver cytochrome detoxification dark chocolate, liver, molasses, forms of hearing loss. Can help period (menstrual) pains in some enzymes, oxygen supply to cells, energy parsley pulses (legumes), red women, anaemia, restless leg syndrome. production in cells, catalase enzyme which meat, shellfish, some types of combats generation of free radicals by peroxides. cheap wine, some green Component of many enzymes. vegetables
Magnesium	Anti-diabetic. Balance and control of calcium, Bitter chocolate, leafy green Can enhance strength gains during athletic training. Can help potassium and sodium ions, vitamins B₁, B₆ and vegetables, nuts, sunflower and chronic fatigue, circulation, fibromyalgia, glaucoma, insulin methionine. Bone development. Energy sesame seeds, soybeans, whole resistance, mood, anxiety, stress-related symptoms, osteoporosis, production. Helps bind calcium to tooth enamel. grains (particularly oats) asthma, insomnia, migraine, gum disease. Can prevent asthma Nerve transmission, muscle contraction and attacks, kidney stones, eclampsia of pregnancy. Can reduce noise-relaxation, protein synthesis, growth and repair. induced hearing loss, high blood pressure, premenstrual symptoms Removal of excess ammonia and acid from body. and period (menstrual) pains, hypoglycaemia, hyperinsulinaemia, cholesterol.

Mineral	Function	Food sources	Benefits
Manganese	Needed for the antioxidant enzyme SOD.	Leafy vegetables, nuts (especially pecans), pulses, tea, whole grains	May reduce epileptic seizures. May enhance action of white blood cells known as natural killer cells and macrophages.
Molybdenum	Detoxification of aldehydes. Haemoglobin, sulphate, taurine and uric acid production. DNA, iron, methionine and cysteine metabolism. Sulphite inactivation.	Beans (especially butterbeans/lima beans). Buckwheat, lentils, liver and other organ meats, split peas, whole grains.	Very little research appears to have been carried out. Has mostly been used to treat Wilson's disease—a copper overload condition.
Selenium	Anti-cancer action. DNA repair. Needed for production of antioxidant enzyme glutathione peroxidase and prostaglandins, immune system, activation of thyroid hormone. Spares vitamin E.	Brazil nuts, fish and shellfish, meat, offal, whole grains	May bring clinical improvement in AIDS, enhance immune function, help asthma, pancreatitis, acne, muscular dystrophy (with vitamin E), rheumatoid– and osteoarthritis, prevent liver cancer, imrove sperm motility, improve function of thyroid and kidneys, reduce risk of contracting viral hepatitis.
Zinc	Acid/alkaline balance, alcohol detoxification, carbon dioxide transport, collagen synthesis, energy metabolism, growth, haemoglobin, hormones, immunity, insulin storage, male fertility, nucleic acid synthesis, numerous enzymes, prostaglandin function, protein digesting enzymes, protein synthesis, SOD (antioxidant enzyme), vitamin A metabolism and distribution.	Eggs, leafy green vegetables, meat, nuts, seafood, seeds, whole grains	May improve abnormally low testosterone in men, sperm count and motility. May help acne, anorexia, birthweight and growth in at-risk babies, healing rate of gastric ulcers, mouth ulcers, management of sickle cell anaemia, thyroid function, tinnitus, white blood cell function, wound healing, enlarged prostate, common cold. May inhibit herpes virus, histamine release, disease activity in rheumatoid arthritis, visual loss in macular degeneration.

Appendix II: Vitamin and mineral deficiency symptoms

Nutrient	Deficiency symptoms
Vitamin A (retinol)	Abnormally poor vision in bad light. Spotty skin (acne). Frequent colds or infections. Dry, scaly skin. Persistent Itching inside ears.
Vitamin B$_1$ (thiamine)	Depression, irritability, fatigue, insomnia, muscle weakness. Burning and tingling in toes and soles.
Vitamin B$_2$ (riboflavin)	Bloodshot, burning, 'gritty' eyes. Cracks and sores in corners of mouth. Dry, cracked, peeling lips. Eyes sensitive to light. Sides of nose red, greasy, scaly. Soreness and burning of lips and tongue.
Vitamin B$_3$ (niacin)	Depression, dermatitis, fatigue, insomnia, irritability, loss of appetite, muscle weakness, red swollen tongue, psychiatric problems.
Vitamin B$_5$ (pantothenic acid)	Burning on soles of feet. Depression, fatigue, loss of appetite, poor muscle co-ordination, weakness, 'wind pains' in intestines.
Vitamin B$_6$ (pyridoxine)	Anaemia, convulsions or fits, inability to remember dreams, insomnia, irritability, kidney stones, morning sickness of pregnancy, nervousness, premenstrual symptoms. Red scaly patches at side of nose and corner of mouth. Skin rashes, especially on forehead.
Vitamin B$_{12}$ (cobalamin)	Agitation, anaemia, disorientation, confusion, unsteadiness, mental derioration, fatigue, psychiatric problems. Increased risk of heart disease due to homocysteine levels rising. Loss of sensation in feet and legs. Sore, smooth tongue.
Folic acid	Anaemia, poor appetite, apathy, birth defects, habitual miscarriage, breathlessness, constipation, fatigue, im-paired growth in children, insomnia, memory impairment, mental confusion, paranoid delusions, reduced immunity, sore tongue, weakness. Increased cancer risk. Increased heart disease risk due to homocysteine levels rising.
Vitamin C (ascorbic acid)	Bleeding gums or loose teeth. Easy bruising and fragile blood vessels. Fatigue, frequent infections.
Vitamin D (calciferol)	Osteoporosis, hearing loss, weak heart and muscle function, higher risk of infections, tumours, autoimmune diseases. Vitamin D deficiency is endemic in colder climates and among those who live mostly indoors or cover their skin when outdoors.
Vitamin E (tocopherol)	Age spots, cataracts, damage to cell membranes, fragility of red blood cells, infertility, muscle weakness, neuro-muscular damage. Possibly auto-immune diseases. Increased risk of cancers and heart disease.

Appendix III: Superfoods
Summary of health benefits

Food	Health benefits
Aubergine (eggplant)	Regarded in Ayurvedic medicine as a prime treatment for female hormonal complaints.
Beans and peas	Good sources of plant protein and one of the few rich plant sources of the amino acid lysine, needed to make carnitine. Lysine helps combat herpes
Blue & purple fruits	Rich in the antioxidant anthocyanin which fights inflammation, keeps blood vessel walls strong and helps prevent damage from pollutants.
Beetroot (beets)	Contains betaine which stimulates liver cell function. Good source of iron. Improves exercise capacity in heart failure.
Brassicas (broccoli, cabbage, etc)	Contain antioxidant indoles which help the liver break down excess oestrogen. Also contain anti-carcinogenic sulphoraphane which stimulates the production of liver detox enzymes.
Carrots	Raw grated carrot taken daily helps to prevent roundworm infestations. Good source of the antioxidant beta carotene.
Celery	Celery juice and celery seed extract help alkalinize the body. Contains coumarin, which helps the body release fluid retention. Can be an effec-tive treatment for arthritis caused by inflammatory fluid pressure on joints.
Chilli pepper	Aids the microcirculation, opening up all tissues to a greater flow of blood and increasing the supply of oxygen and nutrients. Digestive stimulant. Helps prevent intestinal gas.
Cinnamon	Even in small amounts, cinnamon has been found to have an anti-diabetic action.
Coconut oil	Contains anti-viral, anti-fungal lauric acid. Does not raise cholesterol. Aids weight loss by promoting thermogenesis. The body does not handle coconut oil like other fats. It is handled like carbohydrate instead of being converted directly to body fat.
Coriander leaf (cilantro)	May accelerate excretion of the heavy metals mercury, lead and aluminium.
Cucumber	The ground or liquidized seeds can be used to treat tapeworm. The juice is a natural diuretic and soothing for urinary irritations such as cystitis.
Fenugreek seeds	In clinical trials, these have shown an insulin-like effect in the treatment of adult-onset diabetes. Like slippery elm, they can be made into a soothing tea to create a protective coating for an irritated digestive system, and help to lubricate the large intestine.

Garlic	Taken raw, combats many bacteria and parasites. Can help treat bronchitis, dysentery, food poisoning, worm infestations, candidiasis and AIDS-related diarrhoea[212]. Lowers cholesterol and blood pressure.
Ginger	Warming digestive stimulant. Helps prevent flatulence. Often used as a remedy for nausea.
Leafy greens	Rich in lutein, a carotene now being used as a treatment for macular degeneration—a leading cause of blindness.
Lettuce	Very good source of silicon, needed for bones and joints. Wild lettuce was once used as a substitute for opium. The milky juice from the stems of cultivated lettuce also contains natural sedatives.
Mint	Peppermint tea acts as a balm for the digestive system, helping to prevent flatulence and relieving spasms and nausea. Stimulates the flow of bile.
Nuts, sunflower, sesame seeds	Rich in magnesium and essential polyunsaturated oils. Good sources of protein often providing, weight for weight, more protein than animal products
Onions	One of the richest sources of quercetin, a natural anti-histamine with a similar structure to the anti-allergy drug disodium chromoglycate. Quercetin has the most anti-viral activity of all the flavonoids. Onions stimulate the flow of bile, help to reduce cholesterol and may help treat insulin resistance by reducing blood sugar.
Parsley leaf	One of the few good sources of the trace element vanadium, which has similar anti-diabetic properties to chromium. Like celery, parsley is rich in coumarin, which helps eliminate water retention and so can reduce the pain of inflammation.
Pumpkin seeds	Rich in zinc and essential polyunsaturated oils, pumpkin seeds are a good aid to the treatment of enlarged prostate.
Radishes	Radishes help treat the symptoms of the common cold, and also stimulate bile flow. Contain the sulphur compound raphanin, which can help in the treatment of an overactive thyroid gland.
Seaweed	E.g. nori, wakame, hijiki, arame. Rich in iodine, needed to maintain normal levels of female hormones and thyroid hormones.
Soy foods	Help to balance oestrogen. Anti prostate and breast cancer. Reduce cholesterol.
Tomatoes	Rich in lycopene, which helps prevent breast and prostate cancer
Turmeric	Contains powerful antioxidant curcumin. Anti-arthritis, reduces liver inflammation, assists liver drainage and repair. Boosts glutathione[213]. May help in treatment of cancer by inhibiting blood supply to tumours and NF kappa B.

Appendix IV: Using less familiar ingredients

Ingredient	Where To Get It	What It's Good For	How To Use It
Alternative milks (almond, rice, soy, oat etc.)	Health food stores and supermarkets	Alternative to cow's milk	These can replace cow's milk on cereal, in smoothies, puddings, in baking and to make hot chocolate drinks. Soy milk works well in tea. Almond milk is our favourite. Sheep or goat milk, cheese and yoghurt can also be used, but to avoid developing intolerances, try not to use these products every day.
Blue and purple berries (e.g. blueberries, bilberries, blackberries, blackcurrants, elderberries)	Some of these grow wild. You can buy them fresh but they are cheapest from frozen food departments in supermarkets	Rich in flavonoids, vitamin C and minerals	Consume them as they are, or place in an oven-proof casserole dish in a medium oven for 25 minutes or until the fruits split and the juices run. Serve hot or cold. If sweetening is required use a small amount of puréed dates. For more information see the section on Superfoods.
Brown Rice	Supermarkets and health food stores	Rich in B vitamins. A good source of protein	Brown rice is nuttier than white rice and has a different texture. Bring to the boil in twice its volume of water and simmer on the lowest heat until tender (20-25 minutes). Drain in a sieve then immediately put the rice back in the pan. Cover tightly and leave away from the heat for 5 minutes, after which it is ready to serve. Once cold, brown rice can be spread out on an oiled baking tray, frozen, then crumbled into grains and bagged for the freezer.

Buckwheat	Health food stores	Rich in magnesium and in the flavonoid rutin, which helps to build capillary strength	Buckwheat is a grain unrelated to wheat and is a good alternative for people with a gluten or wheat intolerance. Buckwheat flour contains no gluten and is the main ingredient of small Russian pancakes known as blinis. To use as an alternative to rice, toast buckwheat grains in a dry frying pan for 10 minutes over a medium heat. Put in a saucepan with twice their volume of water. Bring to the boil and simmer very gently with the lid on for 15-20 minutes, or until the grains are tender.
Chestnut Flour	Health food stores	Its sweet taste makes it great for cakes and pastries	See the recipes in the book or online
Coconut Oil	Health food stores, oriental grocers and larger supermarkets	Does not raise cholesterol like butter and other animal fats. Is less fattening than other types of fat, as the body does not handle it like fat. Contains lauric acid, which is antifungal and anti-viral.	Use as a replacement for butter in baking and whenever a hard fat is required. Can also be used for frying. Coconut oil is a solid product but is sold in bottles and jars. Virgin coconut oil is more nutritious, but will impart a coconut flavour when used in cooking. To avoid this, you can use refined coconut oil, available from Asian shops and supermarkets. For more information see the section on Superfoods.
Dried Beans, Split Peas, Chickpeas, Dried Peas, Lentils. (Also known as pulses or legumes)	Supermarkets, delicatessens and health food shops	A very cheap source of protein, rich in dietary fibre, B vitamins and minerals	All pulses (legumes) except lentils should be soaked in water before use. Cover with four times their volume in boiling water and leave overnight. Throw away the soaking water, place the pulses, well covered with fresh water, in a pressure cooker, bring to full steam, and cook for 4-10 minutes, depending on size and age. Pressure-cooking breaks down the poisonous lectins found in raw beans. If you do not have a pressure cooker, boil them fast for at least 10 minutes before simmering or slow-cooking. To freeze, allow to cool and follow the same procedure as for frozen brown rice. Lentils need no presoaking. Boil for 20-40 minutes (depending on size) in two and a half times their volume in water. Stir from time to time and add a little more water if they look like drying out.

Gluten Free Flour	Supermarkets, health food stores and online	Commercial blends are sold as plain (all-purpose) flour, self-raising (with raising agent), or bread flour. The plain variety typically consists of 70-75 per cent flour such as rice and buckwheat plus 25-30 per cent starch, usually a combination of potato, corn and tapioca starches. Gluten-free bread flour usually also contains xanthan gum. Cornmeal is also gluten-free and can be used to make cakes and corn bread.	Commercial blends are convenient as a lot of work has gone into finding the best combination of ingredients for different purposes. But you can also experiment with your own blends. Cakes can be made with commeal or fine polenta flour, using a little gram (chickpea) or soy flour instead of egg, to yield a cake-like texture. The mini-muffin recipe in this book uses fruit to add a moist mouth-feel, but this can also be achieved with psyllium husks (from health food stores or online). These can absorb 100 times their weight in water and are very useful for cake and bread-making. You will have to experiment a little to find the perfect amount to use. I suggest starting with two teaspoons psyllium husks per 250 grams (8 ounces) of flour. I buy the whole (unpowdered) husks. Make sure your dough is not too dry as psyllium will quickly absorb moisture. Xanthan gum is said to be a gluten replacer but I have not so far felt the need to use it.
Low-sodium salt	Supermarkets	Typically consist of half to two thirds non-sodium salt and the rest ordinary sodium salt. Recommended by health authorities as too much salt can raise blood pressure	Use like normal salt. You could also use salt substitutes, available online or from pharmacies/drugstores.
Miso	Health food stores, Japanese shops and some supermarkets	A delicious brown stock / broth paste made from fermented soy. Lower in sodium than most stock paste, and very rich in vitamins and minerals. Also contains protein.	Mix with boiling water and use to make gravy and to flavour sauces, soups and stews. Check the product labels as some varieties of miso are made with wheat and barley so are not gluten free. Don't overdo the miso—it does contain salt. Use just enough to get some colour and/or flavour into a dish. Organic miso is best, as soy products are increasingly subject to genetic engineering.

Pumpernickel bread	Supermarkets, health food stores	Wholegrain rye bread with a sweetish, nutty flavour. Buy a brand which contains no yeast or wheat	This bread has a strong flavour and a little goes a long way. Eat with soups and salads, or make into an open sandwich (see the recipes in this book).
Rice Vermicelli and Noodles	Health food stores, oriental grocers and supermarkets	A good alternative to noodles made from wheat	Thin rice noodles are about twice the thickness of vermicelli. Pour boiling water over them and Leave for 2-3 minutes (depending on thickness) then run some cold water into the bowl to stop them cooking before draining the noodles thoroughly in a large sieve. Larger rice noodles, which are flat and ribbon-like, are also available.
Sheep's Milk Yoghurt	Supermarkets and health food stores	A nice creamy alternative to cow's milk yoghurt	Use as normal yoghurt.
Soy Cream	Supermarkets and health food stores	A runny blend of soy protein and oil which can be used as an alternative to dairy single cream	Soy cream is used as a topping for desserts, or can be stirred into soup or gravy to achieve the same effect as single (thin) dairy cream. Look for it under brand names such as Provamel's 'Soy Dream' since some laws prohibit the use of the words milk and cream in association with plant products.
Soy Flour	Health food stores	High in protein. Provides all the benefits of soy foods, including protection against prostate cancer and breast cancer.	A few tablespoons of soy flour can often be used as an alternative to eggs in baking because of its high protein content.

Spelt Flour	Health food stores. Some large supermarkets	An alternative to wholewheat flour, also known as 'ancient wheat'. Spelt is not gluten free but many people who are allergic to wheat are not allergic to spelt	Use exactly as wholewheat flour. You can also buy pasta made from spelt.
Sugar-Free (all-fruit) Jam and Marmalade	Health food stores. Some larger supermarkets also sell the St Dalfour brand	All-fruit jams are made using fruit juice as a sweetener. They contain nothing except fruit and juice	Use as normal jam or to sweeten desserts.
Tamari Sauce	Health food stores	A type of soy sauce, made without using wheat	Use tamari sauce sparingly (since it is salty), to flavour stir-fried dishes. For soups and sauces use wheat-free miso (see above).
Tofu	Supermarkets and health food stores	A good source of protein made from soy—as good as eating meat but with added health benefits	Many of the recipes in this book use tofu. For best results, use the right type. Get to know a particular brand and stick to it if it works. 'Silken' tofu has the consistency of blancmange. It is sold as soft, medium or firm varieties, although the package does not always tell you (a) that the product is silken tofu, or (b) whether it is soft or firm. Don't use silken tofu in these recipes unless specifically instructed. Silken tofu is best for liquidizing and making into mayonnaise and other creamy products. The firmer it is, the less water it contains, and the more water you may have to add to get the finished consistency you want. Standard tofu (e.g. the Cauldron brand found in UK supermarkets) has a 'chewy' consistency and is best for cutting into cubes, dusting with seasoned flour and frying in oil. Can be marinated beforehand for more flavour. It can also be liquidized, poured into moulds, and baked with flavourings. The finished result has a consistency like firm scrambled egg. Tofu needs quite a lot of flavouring to make it tasty.

RECIPE INDEX

RESOURCES

Gluten-free groceries available online
- United Kingdom http://amzn.ws/glutenfree-uk
- United States http://amzn.ws/glutenfree-us

International food terms
- https://en.wikipedia.org/wiki/International_English_food_terms

Weights and measures
- www.convert-me.com

Allergy support organizations
- Allergy UK www.allergyuk.org
- Asthma and Allergy Foundation of America www.aafa.org

Organizations of doctors specializing in naturopathic medicine
- American Academy of Environmental Medicine www.aaemonline.org
- American Association of Naturopathic Physicians www.naturopathic.org
- British Society for Ecological Medicine www.bsem.org.uk
- Orthomolecular.org

Registers of natural medicine practitioners
- American Association of Drugless Practitioners aadp.net
- British Association for Nutritional Therapy bant.org.uk
- Complementary Medicine Association (UK) www.the-cma.org.uk
- Federation of Nutritional Therapy Practitioners (UK) www.fntp.org.uk
- International Institute for Complementary Therapists (Australia) http://myiict.com

Naturopathic nutrition distance learning course with Linda Lazarides
- The School of Modern Naturopathy www.naturostudy.org

Linda's Flat Stomach Secrets

by Linda Lazarides

Have you ever wondered why your waistline keeps expanding as you get older, even though you are exercising the same and not eating any more?

Packed with little-known information, *Linda's Flat Stomach Secrets* explains the five causes of an expanding waistline and includes a comprehensive program and 7-day diet to begin to tackle it. You could lose as much as three inches from your waistline in two months.

Discover

- How to avoid developing obsessive food cravings
- How to rebalance the hormones that control belly fat
- A cool method of walking that powerfully works out your tummy muscles at the same time
- What is intestinal plaque and how it can cause bloating
- A deep-cleansing routine to tackle bloating, gas and water retention.

Linda Lazarides is known for revealing little known but powerful facts about health and weight control. This book is no exception. When Linda was writing it she was shocked to discover that common methods which people believe will help them lose weight can actually put their fat gain hormones into overdrive.

★ ★ ★ ★ ★ **"I found this book very informative and enlightening to say the least "**

Available from Amazon websites and all good bookshops
Ask for ISBN 978-1449976835

The Amino Acid Report

by Linda Lazarides

Maximize the power of vegetarian protein

Protein is one of our most basic needs, but research into how its building blocks, the amino acids, can be combined in different ways to assist health is only just beginning. Linda Lazarides brings you a complete update on the amino acids, what the body uses them for, and the research into their effects on health. Contains much information not published elsewhere.

MEAT, FISH AND DAIRY PRODUCTS ARE NOT ALWAYS
THE BEST SOURCES OF AMINO ACIDS

Read about new amino acid research in chronic fatigue syndrome (M.E.) ❖ Military research by the U.S. Government on amino acids to treat stress ❖ Which aminos are vital to liver detoxification ❖ A new theory about multiple sclerosis ❖ Research into powerful effects of methionine against arthritis and fibromyalgia ❖ How to raise levels of the weight loss aid carnitine with a different, cheaper supplement ❖ The most effective ways to maximize glutathione, which can protect you from Parkinson's disease, chronic fatigue, cancers and autoimmune diseases and can even extend your natural life span ❖ A fallacy exposed: find out why chocolate is not a high-risk food for herpes sufferers, and which really are the high-risk foods ❖ Learn about one of the hottest topics in medicine today—nitric oxide made from the amino acid arginine.

High blood pressure, low sex drive, glaucoma, gout, athletic endurance, depression, schizophrenia, pain, Alzheimer's disease and gall-bladder disease—we now know that all can respond to the right amino acid combinations.

The *Amino Acid Report* brings you comprehensive information on amino acids in seven meat and fish foods and 41 vegetarian foods, including yoghurt, mushrooms, beans, lentils, tofu, potatoes, rice, buckwheat and five different nuts and seeds. Full of charts and tables for you to compare information. The figures are derived from the most comprehensive source in the world—the Agricultural Research Service of the U.S. Department of Agriculture.

A Textbook of Modern Naturopathy

by Linda Lazarides

Covers succinctly a wide variety of important lecture topics in the naturopathic or natural medicine curriculum. It is based on the many articles and factsheets which Linda Lazarides has written for students and practitioners since 1995. Covers topics that every student of holistic health needs to know, including information rarely covered elsewhere: healthy infant nutrition, kidney health, fertility, the microcirculation, the nervous system, metabolic sediment, cell membrane health, the effects of deep-fried foods, moulds (molds) and mycotoxins, and Ayurvedic principles.

Apart from aiming to complement the many excellent publications which are already used as course-books, the author hopes that *A Textbook of Modern Naturopathy* will also play a holistic teaching role—helping to bridge some of the gaps in understanding disease processes and helping the student practitioner to see each problem and each research study in relation to the bigger picture.

Reviews ★ ★ ★ ★ ★

- This is the most complete book I have found on natural health and healing.
- I was so impressed that I have chosen her course to train as a naturopath.
- Very well written book leading one to understand the fundamentals of naturopathy.
- I found much of her input on subjects such as the management of supporting HIV or chronic dysbiosis interesting and provocative.
- Best natural healing book I've found so far .
- Every chapter of this book is well written and easy to read. A tremendous amount of useful information is packed into each chapter. It is one of my favorite books.

Rated 5 stars on goodreads.com and amazon.co.uk

Look for the *Textbook of Modern Naturopathy* on Amazon websites or order ISBN 978-1450549929 from bookstores

Easy Water Retention Diet

by Linda Lazarides

Water retention looks like fat and makes you overweight. But you can't lose it by eating less

Many thousands of people fail to lose weight on a normal, low-calorie diet. This is usually because of hormonal problems (which can be diagnosed by your doctor) or because of water retention.

Until recently, there was no medical treatment for water retention, except diuretics, which have only a temporary effect and can worsen some types of water retention.

Linda Lazarides' water retention diet is a new treatment. It targets seven different types of water retention and makes your kidneys (if they are normal and healthy) release the excess fluid.

You can literally urinate away pounds of your excess body weight

- Have you worked hard to lose weight using conventional methods, and found that you cannot get below a certain weight even if you persevere for months or years?
- Press a fingernail firmly into your thumb pad. Does it stay dented for more than a second or two?
- Press the tip of your finger into the inside of your shin-bone. Can your finger make a dent? Do your ankles ever swell up? Does your shoe size seem to increase as you get older?
- Do your rings sometimes seem not to fit you any more?
- Is your tummy often tight and swollen?
- If you are a woman, do you often suffer from breast tenderness?
- Does your weight ever fluctuate by several pounds within the space of only 24 hours?

If you can answer yes to two or more of these questions you may have hidden water retention

Linda Lazarides' book, the *Easy Water Retention Diet* explains why water tablets and diuretics don't work for idiopathic edema (the most common type of water retention) and could actually make it worse. The book explains the causes of water retention and provides a one-week program offering a significant reduction in idiopathic edema for up to 70 per cent of those who follow the diet.

Available from Amazon websites and all good bookshops
Ask for ISBN 978-1519191472

Made in the USA
Charleston, SC
06 June 2016